EC Consumer Law and Policy

This book is to be returned on
or before the date stamped below

◼ EUROPEAN LAW SERIES ◼

Series Editor:
PROFESSOR JOHN A. USHER

Published Titles

EC Public Procurement Law
CHRISTOPHER BOVIS

International Relations Law of the European Union
DOMINIC McGOLDRICK

EC Insurance Law
ROBERT MERKIN AND ANGUS RODGER

EC Consumer Law and Policy
STEPHEN WEATHERILL

EC Consumer Law and Policy

STEPHEN WEATHERILL

Jean Monnet Professor of European Law
University of Nottingham

LONGMAN

LONDON AND NEW YORK

Addison Wesley Longman Ltd
Edinburgh Gate
Harlow
Essex CM20 2JE
England
and Associated Companies throughout the world.

*Published in the United States of America
by Addison Wesley Longman Inc., New York.*

First published 1997

ISBN 0 582 29162 3 PPR

British Library Cataloguing-in-Publication Data

A catalogue record of this book is
available from the British Library

Library of Congress Cataloging-in-Publication Data

A catalog entry for this title is available from the
Library of Congress

Set by 7

Produced through Longman Malaysia, PA

Contents

Preface

I have always believed that a lot of interesting research has been and is being conducted into EC consumer law and policy. And yet it seems to me that many EC lawyers and students have tended to treat consumer policy as peripheral. Certainly it has suffered badly in comparison with environmental policy, which stole a crucial march by securing insertion as a separate title in the EC Treaty via the Single European Act, while consumer policy was forced to linger on the sidelines until Maastricht, even though consumer policy and environmental policy raise comparable issues of regulatory theory and technique.

I have always suspected that one of the reasons for the relatively small number of active researchers in the EC consumer policy field is the absence of basic introductory works on the subject. (I refuse to believe the reason can lie in any lack of interest in the subject itself!) So I was delighted to have the opportunity to write this book in Longman's new series, edited by John Usher. My purpose in writing this book is to construct a *bridge* between basic EC law principles and the particular context in which they are applied in consumer policy. To this end, I assume a basic grasp of the pattern of the EC legal order, but do not assume any advanced knowledge. So the book should be readily accessible to anyone who has followed an introductory EC law course, covering institutional and constitutional law and the basic framework of trade law. This is a short book only, so I do not immerse the reader in a highly technical research agenda, but I do make clear where the difficult areas requiring further theoretical and empirical analysis lie, and naturally I provide plenty of sources of further reading. The book should be perfectly intelligible on its own, although the reader could usefully have the texts of relevant Treaty provisions, Directives and Resolutions to hand.

Any book on 'consumer law', whether national or transnational, has to make difficult choices about its subject matter. Consumer law is notoriously fuzzy-edged. I have picked the areas which I think would normally be regarded as the core of consumer policy. Separate treatment of detailed areas such as food and pharmaceuticals has been omitted, with reluctance, largely because to include it would have left me with too much detailed explanation which would have precluded discussion of policy. Most of all, I have tried to trace the trends in the evolution of consumer policy in the belief that they illustrate much about the evolution of the EC generally.

I owe thanks to many people, most of all, in the EC consumer field, to Geoffrey Woodroffe, Hans Micklitz and Norbert Reich. I also acknowledge with gratitude financial support for aspects of my research in these areas provided by a Small Personal Research Grant made by the British Academy and by the Butterworths Fund for European Exchanges administered by the Society for Public Teachers of Law.

Stephen Weatherill
March 1997

General Editor's Preface

The Longman European Law Series is the first comprehensive series of topic-based books on EC Law aimed specifically at a student readership, though it is hoped that they will also be found useful by academic colleagues and interested practitioners. It has become more and more difficult for a single course or a single book to deal comprehensively with all the major topics of Community law, and the intention of this series is to enable students and teachers to 'mix and match' topics which they find to be of interest; it may also be hoped that the publication of this series will encourage the study of areas of Community law which have historically been neglected in degree courses. However, while the series may have a student readership in mind, the authors have been encouraged to take an academic and critical approach, placing each topic in its overall Community context, and also in its socio-economic and political context where relevant.

I am delighted that Professor Weatherill has agreed to write one of the first books in the series. Professor Weatherill is well-known both as a writer on Community law in general and as a specialist in EC Consumer Law, an area in which he has many years of research experience. EC Consumer Law is a topic of interest in its substance, some aspects of which show Community law affecting core areas of private law. It is also of interest institutionally, in the development through general Treaty powers of a new policy, which has eventually been recognised in an express provision of the EC Treaty as amended at Maastricht. As Professor Weatherill states in his preface, his purpose is to construct a bridge between basic EC law principles and the particular context in which they are applied in consumer policy.

John A. Usher
March 1997

Table of Cases

xi

Table of Legislation

CHAPTER ONE

The evolution of Community consumer policy

The challenge of EC consumer policy

> Consumer protection ... has a bearing on what is probably the
> most central issue of European economic integration for it brings
> into very sharp relief the dialectics of open borders, protectionism,
> and bona fide intervention of the Member State to protect
> legitimate societal values and goals even if at the expense of
> interrupting the free flow of goods on which the idea of a common
> marketplace is postulated. To understand the problematics of
> consumer protection in the common market context is to
> understand the core issue of European market integration.[1]

This observation still holds true a decade – and two formal
revisions of the EC Treaty – later. In fact, the capacity of
consumer policy to provide insights into some of the fundamental
tensions that beset the evolution of the Community is today
enhanced. At Maastricht, it was agreed to add to the Treaty for
the first time an explicit provision empowering Community
action in the consumer protection field. The relationship between
this 'positive' commitment to market regulation at Community
level and the 'negative' emphasis on removing national laws that
act as trade barriers in pursuit of market integration remains
obscure. It is not overstating the case to claim that striking the
balance between deregulation and re-regulation of the
Community market is the most controversial economic issue
facing the Community today. Social policy has been the most
high-profile battleground, but consumer policy, too, is a richly
illustrative area of inquiry.

---

1. T. Bourgoignie and D. Trubek, *Consumer Law, Common Markets and
Federalism* (Berlin, De Gruyter, 1987), p. vi.

Study of EC consumer policy requires examination of both the absolute scope of Community competence and the scope of Community competence relative to that of the member states, which, in the guise of the principle of subsidiarity, has generated much controversy in political debate during the 1990s. In judging the appropriate intensity of regulation required in the evolving European market, it is perilously simplistic to reduce the argument to 'competition between regulators' versus the 'level playing field'. Nevertheless, with caution in mind, those slogans are of value in sketching the contours of a debate which will be pursued in more depth throughout this book. There is a beguiling simplicity to the notion that a common market should be regulated by common rules. Yet today the quest to establish such a pattern is under increasing strain. In part this is attributable to the geographic and functional expansion of the EC, which renders agreement increasingly hard to achieve. The range of interests at stake in the EC cannot be readily reduced to a single agreed norm. More fundamentally, there is an increasingly voiced case against harmonization. Better, it is said by some sources, to allow traders access to the markets of all member states subject only to compliance with the rules of their home state. The host state could retain a regulatory regime different from other states, but could not use those regulatory differences as a basis for denying access to an out-of-state trader. This would be a system of mutual recognition of national rules. Firms could then choose where to locate in order to supply the whole market, influenced by prevailing regulatory strategies. Firms – the market – would select which regulatory regime suited them best. It can readily be appreciated that this approach not only downplays the need for harmonization and a level playing field, but in fact portrays harmonization as an undesirable suppression of a market in which regulators compete for customers. The debate is not only directed at the internal aspects of EC policy; it is also argued that, externally, the EC will lose its competitive position if it locks itself into a single internal standard.

Beyond debate about the appropriate reach of harmonization as a basis for a level commercial playing field, there are arguments about the extent to which regulation at Community level is needed for reasons other than ironing out differences between national legal systems. It is argued that a wider market needs a wider regulatory system to achieve, loosely, social justice, not just an integrated free market. The role of the provisions on Economic and Social Cohesion[2] deserve attention from this perspective, but all the common policies can be fitted within this analytical framework. No one doubts that the EC is deregulatory – knocking down national regulations that impede trade is a key part of its economic success – but there is plenty of doubt about the appropriate intensity of European-wide *re*-regulation.

This is an inevitably superficial overview of a key philosophical debate about the Community's future.[3] In seeking to reconcile preferences for 'competition between regulators' (most closely associated with the Thatcher/Major administrations in the UK) with the 'level playing field', the EC is wavering between a constructive adjustment to new patterns of growth to which all members need not necessarily subscribe and, on a gloomier interpretation, patterns of fragmentation that are corrosive of past success and future viability. Such 'variable geometry' challenges many of the assumptions about the role of Community regulatory activity. As the EC pursues its path of geographic and functional expansion, marked by periodic intergovernmental conferences, the debate about how far to move beyond deregulation and market liberalization towards patterns of substantive and institutional re-regulation (in common or not) is becoming increasingly acute.

These critical issues are readily applicable to patterns of development of consumer policy. It is certainly true that consumer policy has not attracted the level of political friction that may be observed in the field of, most of all, social policy, where the UK secured a pattern at Maastricht which allows it to compete with (the so far small number of) measures adopted in common by the other fourteen member states under the Protocol-plus-Agreement.[4] To an extent, the consumer policy field invites a fresher inquiry, uncontaminated by the vitriol surrounding the social policy debate. But, from the deregulatory, 'competition between regulators' quarter emanates severe

---

2. Articles 130a–e, introduced by the Single European Act, and expanded at Maastricht.
3. Cf. N. Reich, 'Competition Between Legal Orders: A New Paradigm of EC Law' 29 CMLRev 861 (1992).
4. E. Whiteford, 'Social Policy after Maastricht', 18 ELRev 202 (1993); C. Barnard and S. Deakin, 'Social Policy in Search of a Role' in Caiger and Floudas, *1996 Onwards* (Chichester, Wiley Chancery, 1996).

scepticism about whether the EC should even have a consumer policy at all. An emphasis on market deregulation breeds opposition to active regulatory policies at Community level; such a perspective treats EC consumer policy as anti-competitive. One might be tempted to suppose that supporters of such a viewpoint were routed at Maastricht, where an explicit consumer protection Title was inserted into the EC Treaty. However, the simultaneous inclusion of the subsidiarity principle guaranteed a persisting debate about the appropriate intensity of Community intervention, and, in practice, the new Title has been little used since the Union Treaty entered into force on 1 November 1993.

Debates which are conducted under the slogans of variable geometry, competition between regulators and subsidiarity all relate to the critical question of the Community's competence and the impact of Community action on residual member state powers. The debates persist within the framework of the Intergovernmental Conference (IGC) which commenced in Turin in March 1996, and the intractable nature of the issues ensures a high profile during and beyond the IGC. Indeed, an appreciation that the argument is re-fuelled by the tensions brought to the Community polity by functional and geographic expansion confirms that these are issues that will command interest for many years to come, as the Community continues to evolve. The purpose of this book is to show that consumer policy serves as a window on wider policy issues in the EC legal order, while remaining of interest in its own right.[5]

Consumer policy under the Treaty of Rome

The Treaty of Rome was agreed in 1957 and entered into force in 1958. It contains only four explicit references to the consumer. Article 39 contains a list of five objectives of the common agricultural policy, the fifth of which is 'to ensure that supplies reach consumers at reasonable prices'. Article 40 requires that the common organization of agricultural markets shall exclude 'any discrimination between producers or consumers within the Community'. Under Article 85(3), one of the conditions for exempting an agreement between firms from the prohibition of

---

5. Cf. N. Reich, *Europäisches Verbraucherrecht* (Baden-Baden: Nomos, 3rd edn, 1996).

4

Article 85(1) is the requirement that it allow consumers 'a fair share of the resulting benefit'. Article 86 provides an illustrative list of abusive conduct perpetrated by dominant firms, including 'limiting production, markets or technical development to the prejudice of consumers'. None of these explicit references to the consumer represents an attempt to develop a sophisticated structure of consumer rights or interests. In fact, the assumption of the original Treaty pattern is that the consumer will benefit from the process of integration through the enjoyment of a more efficient market, which will yield more competition, allowing wider choice, lower prices and higher quality products and services. The substantive provisions of the Treaty, such as those designed to remove barriers to the free circulation of goods, persons and services (Articles 30, 48 and 59, respectively), are provisions designed indirectly to improve the lot of the consumer. These Treaty provisions are further examined from this perspective in Chapter 2. Moreover, there existed no explicit basis in the original Treaty for making Community legislation in the area of consumer protection and, since the Community can act only in areas in which it is attributed powers by the Treaty, legislative action affecting the consumer could only be indirect.

However, despite this barren Treaty background, which persisted unchanged until the entry into force of the Single European Act in 1987, a type of 'EC consumer policy' took shape through two routes. The first route was the harmonization of national laws in the field of consumer protection, leading to a form of 'indirect' consumer policy at Community level. The second was through 'soft law' initiatives in the field. Gradual expansion of Community activity beyond narrowly defined Treaty limitations has been a characteristic feature of the evolution of the Community since its inception.[6]

A theme of this book is exploration of the extent to which it is possible to talk of a European consumer law and policy in spite of this unfavourable background in the Treaty. The thesis of this book holds that it is possible to identify notions of the role of the consumer through examination of Community judicial and legislative activity. It has been necessary for the institutions to

---

[6.] J. Weiler, 'The Transformation of Europe' 100 Yale LJ 2403 (1991); R. Dehousse, 'Community Competence: Are there Limits to Growth?' in R. Dehousse (ed.) *Europe after Maastricht* (Munich, Law Books, 1994).

elaborate their own perceptions of the consumer in order to develop a range of other Community policies, most notably, but not exclusively, the process of building an integrated market. In this sense, the shaping of an 'EC consumer policy' has not been a story of opportunistic theft of member state competences by the Community institutions, but rather simply an inevitable part of the evolution of the Community towards its current *sui generis* status as something more than a market, but less than a state.

Harmonization legislation as an indirect consumer policy

Article 100 of the Treaty provides '. . . for the approximation of such provisions laid down by law, regulation or administrative action in member states as directly affect the establishment or functioning of the common market'. This legislative power is subject to a requirement of unanimity in the Council.

The existence of different consumer protection rules in different member states has been viewed as a sufficient basis for introducing harmonized Community rules based on Article 100. Diversity between national regimes obstructs market integration, thereby providing a rationale for harmonization at Community level. In this way, a body of Community rules impinging on consumer protection has been adopted indirectly as part of the process of market integration.

After the entry into force of the Single European Act in 1987, a new provision, Article 100a, began to be used to harmonize national laws in the field of, inter alia, consumer protection. Article 100a(1) provides for the adoption of measures '. . . for the approximation of the provisions laid down by law, regulation or administrative action in member states which have as their object the establishing and functioning of the internal market'. This provision has largely superseded Article 100 as an instrument of harmonization. Despite the reference to the internal market in Article 100a, in contrast to the common market mentioned in Article 100, the rationale for Community action is comparable under both provisions. Variation between national laws impedes market integration, prompting a need for harmonization at Community level. Here, too, a package of Community consumer protection legislation has evolved indirectly. The critical difference between Articles 100 and 100a lies not in their substance but in the applicable legislative procedure. Since the amendments made by the Treaty on European Union, measures are made under Article 100a by Council and Parliament, employing the Article 189b 'co-decision' procedure; but, more significant still, the applicable voting rule in Council is qualified majority voting (QMV). QMV is based on the allocation of weighted votes to member states according to their population, with a threshold figure which must be crossed before a measure is deemed adopted by QMV. The key point is that a single state is unable to block adoption of a measure subject to QMV in Council. A minority of three or more dissentient states (depending on their identity) must be assembled to prevent the adoption of an initiative.[7] This contrasts starkly with the unanimity requirement under Article 100. The absence of any national veto under Article 100a has, as was intended at the time of the drafting of the Single European Act, ensured the vitality of that provision as a basis for making a large number of measures associated with the process of completion of the internal market, a task which was widely advertised as subject to a deadline at the end of 1992 but which, in fact, for all the symbolic and legal significance of that date, remains an evolving process. Measures affecting consumer protection are part of the '1992 package'.

Other Treaty provisions have also been used as bases for the adoption of measures which impinge on the consumer interest. Articles 57(2) and 66 EC permit the adoption of measures designed to liberalize the free circulation of persons and services. That process is part of the impetus towards market integration from which the consumer is the ultimate beneficiary. Accordingly, such harmonization, yielding, for example, liberalization in markets for financial services, also counts as an indirect aspect of EC consumer law and policy.

Article 235, the broadest of all bases for action provided by the Treaty, has also been employed to make legislation relevant to consumer protection. Article 235 provides that '[i]f action by the Community should prove necessary to attain, in the course of the operation of the common market, one of the objectives of the Community and this Treaty has not provided the necessary powers',

---

[7.] S. Weatherill and P. Beaumont, *EC Law* (London, Penguin Books, 2nd edition, 1995), chs 3, 5.

then the Council is empowered to act. Like Article 100, Article 235 is and always has been subject to a requirement of unanimity in Council. Where it was not thought possible to use a more specific legal base on its own, Article 235 has on occasion provided a residuary base for the adoption of measures affecting the consumer.

Harmonization of national laws by Community legislation involves the establishment of a common EC rule governing the sector throughout the territory of the Community. The interest underlying the permissible national rules is protected at EC level, but free trade is facilitated because protection is achieved according to a common EC standard, which irons out differences between national systems. The Community has taken over the job of setting legal standards of protection, a process of both deregulation (in that many different systems are reduced to one), but also re-regulation (in that the Community becomes the responsible regulatory authority).

Harmonization of laws secures market integration; and, constitutionally, that appears to be the whole point of legislation made under Articles 100 and 100a. But harmonization also establishes regulatory standards at Community level – indirectly, perhaps, but unavoidably. The consumer interest is part of the assessment of the shaping of measures adopted under Articles 100 and 100a, so a Community consumer policy emerges as a by-product of market integration. This will be traced in several areas in the course of this book. The Community institutions were inevitably drawn into a process of identification of the nature of the consumer interest even though the pre-Maastricht Treaty avoided any explicit elaboration of the nature and purpose of consumer protection.

This book takes as a principal theme the indirect growth of EC consumer policy. It assumes that it is too simplistic to assert a sustainably neat divide between the Community's interest in market integration and the role of the member states in matters of market regulation in the sphere of consumer protection. The Community's role has inevitably spread, blurring this initially appealing division of function. The Community has developed a form of consumer policy, both in judging the validity of national consumer laws which impede trade (the subject matter of Chapter 2 of this book) and also through the need to elaborate the substantive content of legislative harmonization, in particular under Articles 100 and 100a. So, despite occasional complaint that the Community's harmonization programme strayed beyond its proper Treaty limits,[8] it is ,hard to see how an effective legislative programme for the construction of an internal market could avoid exerting this type of impact on national law.[9] Nevertheless, this approach must be capable of withstanding the objection that even though harmonization might have impinged on consumer law, it has not done so in any coherent fashion. The measures that will be reviewed in this book disclose a range of different techniques and assumptions. It must be considered whether the absence of any firmly established constitutional basis for a Community consumer protection policy has caused such measures as have been made to have no thematic linkage with each other other than the fact that they happen to affect the consumer interest. There are also institutional reasons for scepticism about the viability of treating consumer policy as distinctive; it was as late as 1995 before a separate Directorate-General within the Commission took charge of consumer policy. Looking ahead, an unanswered question raised by the Maastricht Treaty amendments centres on the extent to which Community consumer policy, freed from its necessary concealment within internal market policy by the new Article 129a, can or should develop an autonomous regulatory character. In summary, one must be wary of *overstating* the case for treating the Community as possessing a thematically coherent consumer policy. This is an issue which will be revisited in the concluding chapter.

Soft law: the first two resolutions

The 'soft law' contribution to the rise of EC consumer protection occurred as part of general trends in Community policy making in the early 1970s. At this time, following the largely successful transitional period – within which many obvious trade barriers had been first reduced and then eliminated in accordance with timetables set out within the Treaty – political importance was increasingly attached to widening the Community's focus beyond

---

8. House of Lords Select Committee on the European Communities (22nd Report) (1977–78).
9. G. Close, 'The Legal Basis for the Consumer Protection Programme of the EEC and Priorities for Action' 8 ELRev 221 (1983); L. Krämer, *EEC Consumer Law* (Brussels, Story Scientia, 1986).

economic integration alone. At the 'Paris Summit' in October 1972 the member states expressed a general desire to broaden the appeal of the Community beyond economic affairs and into the social sphere. As one element in this policy, the heads of state and government called for the submission of a programme of consumer protection policy.

The soft law initiative that emerged from this new political atmosphere was the first in a lengthy series which continues today. It was the Council Resolution of 14 April 1975 on a preliminary programme of the European Economic Community for a consumer protection and information policy.[10] This Resolution constituted the formal inauguration of a consumer protection and information policy for the Community. The Annex, a 'Preliminary Programme of the European Economic Community for a Consumer Protection and Information Policy', provides a relatively extended assertion of the place of the consumer interest in Community law. It is a relatively ambitious agenda, built on the perception that the consumer interest represents a distinctive element in society. In Point 3, it is explained that –

> [t]he consumer is no longer seen merely as a purchaser and user of goods and services for personal, family or group purposes but also as a person concerned with the various facets of society which may affect him directly or indirectly as a consumer.

Point 3 encapsulates consumer interests in a statement of five basic rights:

(a) the right to protection of health and safety;
(b) the right to protection of economic interests;
(c) the right of redress;
(d) the right to information and education;
(e) the right of representation (the right to be heard).

The assertion of this notion of consumer 'rights' in the Resolution, which is transparently inspired by US President Kennedy's similar declaration in March 1962, suggests an acceptance by the Council that the consumer interest transcends a purely economic, open-border focus. However, Point 4 provides an immediate reminder that, in conformity with the formal terms

10. OJ 1975 C92/1.

of the EC Treaty, there is no consumer protection policy which exists independently of other Community policies. Consumer policy will be amplified '. . . by action under specific Community policies such as the economic, common agricultural, social, environment, transport and energy policies as well as by the approximation of laws, all of which affect the consumer's position . . .'

Action designed to achieve consumer protection *per se* cannot be pursued in the absence of a separate consumer protection Title in the Treaty, a constitutional deficiency which persisted until Maastricht. Appendix 2 to the Resolution, 'A Selection of Council Directives of Interest to Consumers', confirms the limited progress made. The list is largely devoted to measures in the field of harmonization of laws concerning foodstuffs, animal health, textiles and motor vehicles. Important though such measures may be, they do not come close even to a glimpse of a comprehensive consumer policy. Therefore, the first Council Resolution on a preliminary programme for a consumer protection and information policy reveals a gap between policy aspiration and available constitutional foundation.

The 1975 Resolution on the preliminary programme was followed in 1981 by the Council Resolution of 19 May 1981 on a second programme of the European Economic Community for a consumer protection and information policy.[11] The 1981 Resolution is based on the same essential premises as those which underlie the first Resolution. It repeats the five basic rights. The Resolution expresses a priority for action in the field of the quality of goods and services, the conditions affecting their supply and the provisions of information about them. It also places rather firmer emphasis than the first Resolution on improving consultation between consumer representatives, producers and distributors.

These soft law initiatives were of significance in the gradual development of a political atmosphere conducive to recognition of the distinctive function that may be performed by consumer policy. Moreover, although Article 189 EC makes it plain that Resolutions are not binding legislative acts, such initiatives are not wholly devoid of legal effect. For example, the Court has drawn on the emphasis placed on the value of providing

---

[11]. OJ 1981 C133/1.

information to the consumer in the 1981 Resolution in interpreting Article 30 in the context of a national measure restricting the provision of information to consumers.[12] Soft law has a real significance in patterns of policy development in the consumer field and beyond. Nevertheless, legislative elaboration of EC consumer policy *per se* remained foreclosed by the absence of any explicit base in the Treaty.

The Single European Act and consumer policy

From the middle of the 1980s, the EC's focus was the completion of the internal market by the end of 1992.[13] This project was presented as a method of accelerating integration in order to realize the substantial economic benefits which were suppressed by the fragmented pattern of 'non-Europe'. The advantages that were identified, most prominently in the Cecchini Report,[14] were based on deeper market integration as a stimulus to competition and an encouragement to specialization, permitting the realization of economies of scale. The process was generally designed to achieve enhanced economic efficiency. Theory assumes that the ultimate beneficiary in such a process will be the consumer as the recipient of a wider choice of goods and services at a higher quality level and a lower price level. To this extent, the perceived advantages of the internal market for the consumer were comparable to those already expected to flow from the programme designed to construct a common market. The consumer maintained a position as the assumed, indirect beneficiary of the process.

The Single European Act (SEA), which entered into force in 1987, made a number of changes to the pattern of the original Treaty of Rome which had been agreed 30 years previously. Among other things, the SEA conferred new formal competences on the Community in areas such as environmental protection and research and development. However, consumer protection did not figure in the list of additions to the Community's functional

---

12. Case C-362/88 *GB-INNO v CCL*, examined in Chapter 2.
13. The pattern of the project was initially advanced in the Commission's 'White Paper' on Completing the Internal Market, COM (85) 310.
14. Summarized in P. Cecchini, *The European Challenge: 1992, the Benefits of a Single Market* (Aldershot, Wildwood House, 1988).

competence. No explicit reference to a strategy for promoting the consumer interest was added to the Treaty by the SEA.

According to the Commission's strategy for completing the internal market, the removal of remaining obstacles to trade was to be achieved by effective application of the existing *acquis communautaire*, accompanied by the adoption of some 300 legislative measures, a figure subsequently slightly reduced. These measures were required to eliminate barriers to trade which remained lawful under primary Community law. This programme promised a reinvigoration of the Community's activity. However, the intense legislative output required of the political institutions of the Community would have been unattainable under a Treaty structure favouring unanimous voting. Indeed, prior to the SEA, the Community suffered from a serious legislative log-jam, caused by the need to proceed at the pace of the most reluctant member, which severely stifled progress. Accordingly, as mentioned above, a key element in the process of construction of the internal market was the insertion into the Treaty of Article 100a, which has in practice replaced Article 100 as the principal vehicle for the harmonization of laws. Article 100a requires only a qualified majority vote in Council, in contrast to the obstructive insistence on unanimity under Article 100. Removal of the national veto available under Article 100 was critical to the practical realization of the internal market.

It is also worth noting that Article 100a broadened the type of legal act that can be used for the purpose of harmonization. Whereas Article 100 permits the making of Directives alone, Article 100a allows 'measures' to be made. Accordingly, although there has been a long-standing preference for the Directive in the sphere of law making affecting consumer policy, there has been since 1987 constitutional scope for adoption of, inter alia, a Regulation. Nevertheless, in practice, the Directive typically remains the more appropriate instrument for consumer policy making, as the Community seeks to construct a Community framework built on and strengthened by existing, well-established national structures. It will be seen in this book that the pattern of Community consumer policy largely comprises Directives and soft law instruments such as Recommendations.

The constitutional breakthrough to QMV in connection with harmonization legislation presented to Council was vital to the ability of Article 100a to serve as a cornerstone of the internal market project. Article 100a has indeed proved fundamental in the construction of a legislative framework for the internal market; a number of measures examined in this book are based on Article 100a. Nevertheless, even though one might suppose that states were prepared to surrender a veto they valued in some areas in anticipation of greater gains consequent on other states losing their veto in other areas, it was judged politically necessary to include qualifications to the basic rule of QMV in Council asserted in Article 100a(1). By virtue of Article 100a(2), 'fiscal provisions, . . . those relating to the free movement of persons [and] . . . those relating to the rights and interests of employed persons' lie beyond the scope of Article 100a and the possibility of adoption thereunder by QMV. The provisions of Articles 100a(3) and (4) are more subtle, and of more direct significance to consumer policy. However, before they are examined, it is important to provide some explanation of the impact of Community legislative activity on national competence, for this is of significance in gauging the attitude of the member states to the new burst of legislative activity stimulated by the Single European Act.

Pre-emption

Article 100a opened up prospects for an acceleration in the development of indirect consumer protection policy through the possibility that harmonized standards of consumer protection could be put in place at Community level without unanimous support among the member states. But, to put it bluntly, this created a fear at national level that regulation might be sacrificed to integration. After all, the harmonization of laws in pursuit of a level playing field is a process which makes no particular demands of the content of those rules. Whether the harmonized standard is based on stringent protective standards or on a prohibition of any public intervention whatsoever is irrelevant from the narrow perspective of putting all traders throughout the Community on the same footing. All that matters is that the rule shall be common to all states. An awareness that this could result in a minority of states with high standards of protection being forced to dilute their regimes down to a harmonized compromise standard prompted a readiness to re-examine the constitutional impact of Community legislation on national competence in the relevant field.

In the light of the rationale for harmonization activity as a means of securing market integration, the simple constitutional assumption would seem to be that once the Community acts, its rules must apply to the exclusion of national norms in the field in question. The Community rule secures protection of the interests underlying the national rules at Community level; and free trade is opened up, because all traders adhere to the same, common rule wherever they are based. The national rules are replaced by the Community law. Classic federalist jargon holds that the adoption of a Community rule 'pre-empts' national competence. The field is occupied by the Community, and barred to national law making.[15] Such pre-emption of national law by Community rules appears seductively necessary as a means of ensuring that the playing field is truly levelled by the Community rule. In the absence of a rule that Community legislation occupies the field to the exclusion of national rules, variation between national regimes would persist and free trade would be compromised. In many instances of interpretation of harmonization legislation, the European Court has found that the Community rule precludes national rules setting different standards. For example, in *Commission v UK*, the so-called 'Dim-Dip' case,[16] the UK had introduced a requirement that all new vehicles should carry dim-dip lights, although such devices were not listed in a relevant Directive. In consequence, the importation into the UK of vehicles made in other member states according to the specifications set out in the Directive was impeded. The Court held that the Directive was exhaustive as regards the lighting devices which might be made compulsory for motor vehicles. The UK was no longer competent to introduce extra requirements, given the comprehensive coverage achieved under the Directive. Were it true that (as the UK argued) dim-dip devices improved road safety, then the UK could secure their introduction by persuading its partners to adjust the terms of the Directive. But it was pre-empted from acting unilaterally.

Pre-emption has a powerful attraction as a means of building a constitutional framework for an integrated market on which traders may confidently rely. Yet pre-emption has drawbacks. It obstructs the possibility of innovation. The only way to change

---

15. Weatherill and Beaumont, *EC Law*, pp. 478–85.
16. Case 60/86 [1988] ECR 3921.

the rule is through the laborious processes of the Community legislative machinery. There is at least a view that Community rules should allow more flexibility to individual member states wishing to test new techniques. The 'Dim-Dip' case is exemplary; the UK's submissions were not rejected after an examination of the alleged merit of the new devices but, rather, simply because it was constitutionally impermissible to introduce rules that imposed restrictions extending beyond those laid down in the Community measure. This leads on to the familiar complaint that the Community's legal structure may subordinate market rĕgulation to market integration; that the insistence on reliable groundrules for free trade may override concerns in particular cases for extra levels of market regulation, inter alia, to protect the consumer. From this perspective, it is sometimes argued that the rules of pre-emption place an undue emphasis on treating national rules of market regulation simply as barriers to trade, instead of appraising them in their true, broader social function. A different, more pragmatic criticism of 'classic pre-emption' points out that states are likely to be fearful of the radical loss of competence that flows from agreement in Council on a measure that totally pre-empts national competence, especially given that the principles of direct effect and supremacy ensure that in the EC a state cannot lightly disregard a rule once agreed.[17] This may breed caution in Council at the stage of negotiating draft legislation, leading to blockages in the process.

Such considerations have led to increasing trends of departure from the classic, clean-cut principles of pre-emption.[18] States are allowed greater leeway. The field of legislation affecting consumer protection provides a number of clear examples of a process whereby competence is shared between states and Community, even after the Community has legislated in a field. This is important in any examination of the pattern of EC consumer policy, but it also serves to illuminate broader questions of tension in the relationship between state powers and Community powers. Many of the awkward aspects of pre-emption discussed in the previous paragraph become profoundly more awkward as the Community proceeds along the path of

---

17. Cf. Case 148/78 *Pubblico Ministero v Ratti* [1979] ECR 1629.
18. E. Cross, 'Pre-emption of Member State Law in the European Economic Community: A Framework for Analysis' 29 CMLRev 447 (1992); S. Weatherill, *Law and Integration in the European Union* (Oxford, OUP, 1995), ch.5.

geographic and functional expansion. Slippage away from 'one rule for all' has a certain inevitability in the expanded modern Community, but abandoning classic pre-emption has inevitable costs in the loss of reliability in the common legal pattern for the Community.

The 'minimum harmonization' formula is common in many consumer protection Directives.[19] Rather than setting a single Community rule as both floor and ceiling, the Community measure acts as a floor, but the ceiling is set only by primary Community law. So, for example, member states must put in place the rules against misleading advertising that are found in Directive 84/450, but they may maintain or introduce stricter rules provided that such rules do not come into conflict with, inter alia, rules governing the free movement of goods in Article 30 EC (Chapter 6). The attraction of the minimum formula is strong in the area of consumer policy, not least because it avoids the risk that Community measures may suppress long-established and well-developed national initiatives. Minimum harmonization has the capacity to reflect the reality of cultural heterogeneity between the member states. Yet it also runs the risk of acquiescing in the fragmentation of the Community market as states make different choices about the level at which they will pitch their rules above the required minimum.

At the time of the negotiation of the SEA, concern to provide that state competence in areas covered by measures made by QMV under Article 100a would not be totally excluded led to the inclusion of Articles 100a(3) and (4).

The nature and purpose of Articles 100a(3) and (4)

Article 100a(3) provides that 'The Commission, in its proposals envisaged in paragraph 1 concerning health, safety, environmental protection and consumer protection, will take as a base a high level of protection'. This is significant, first of all, for the addition it makes to the relatively small number of Treaty provisions which include explicit reference to the consumer. It reflects awareness of the risk that the drive for common

---

[19.] K. Mortelmans, 'Minimum Harmonisation and Consumer Law' European Consumer Law Journal 2 (1988).

standards could cause a reduction in existing standards in some states. The provision is plainly designed to allay fears that the Community rules may undercut existing national standards of, inter alia, consumer protection. Indeed, since the entry into force of the SEA, a number of measures made on the basis of Article 100a that touch consumer protection have included an explanation of their content in the light of Article 100a(3). For example, Directive 90/88, made under Article 100a and amending Directive 87/102 in the field of consumer credit, includes in its Recitals an explicit reference to the desirability of ensuring 'that consumers benefit from a high level of protection' (Chapter 3). To an extent, Article 100a(3) represents a deepening of the link between internal market policy and consumer protection. After the SEA, consumer protection remains an indirect element in the harmonization programme, but by virtue of the impact of Article 100a(3) the linkage has become *less* indirect.

Article 100a(3) makes a contribution to dictating the *content* of measures that emerge from the harmonization process. Harmonization policy should not simply be a matter of agreeing common rules irrespective of content. However, the textual limitations of Article 100a(3) as a guarantee of high standards should be noted. It is addressed to the Commission, not to the Council, which is the institution (with the Parliament, since Maastricht) responsible for the adoption of the legislation. Moreover, Article 100a(3) requires only that a high level of protection be taken 'as a base', which implies that it may be adjusted downwards in subsequent negotiation. In any event, the notion of a 'high level' lacks precision and its interpretation may vary between member states. The justiciability of Article 100a(3) is not clear and has never been tested. Its flavour is more political aspiration than independently enforceable legal norm.

At the institutional level, one might add that neither Article 100a(3) nor any other provision in the post-SEA Treaty provides for an explicit consumer input into the shaping of proposals. The Commission has endeavoured to establish methods of consumer input through a series of differently constituted consumer representative bodies.[20] This process is of some value, but the

---

[20.] The Consumers' Consultative Committee, Dec.73/306/EEC, OJ 1973 L283/18, the Consumers' Consultative Council, Dec.90/55/EEC, OJ 1990 L38/40, (from 1995, and slimmed down to improve flexibility and speed) the Consumer Committee, Dec.95/260 OJ 1995 L162/37.

consumer voice within the Commission may be drowned by those of other, less diffuse, interest groups, especially in the commercial sphere. And the Commission itself does not enjoy any direct legislative power in fields close to consumer policy.

Article 100a(4) represents an even more direct assertion of the fear at national level of the consequences of yielding legislative competence to the Community under a QMV regime based on the abandonment of the national veto.

> If, after the adoption of a harmonization measure by the Council acting by a qualified majority, a member state deems it necessary to apply national provisions on grounds of major needs referred to in Article 36, or relating to protection of the environment or the working environment, it shall notify the Commission of these provisions.
>
> The Commission shall confirm the provisions involved after having verified that they are not a means of arbitrary discrimination or a disguised restriction on trade between member states.
>
> By way of derogation from the procedure laid down in Articles 169 and 170, the Commission or any member state may bring the matter directly before the Court of Justice if it considers that another member state is making improper use of the powers provided for in this Article.

Article 100a(4) has similarities to Article 100a(3) in its manifestation of national fear about the propensity of Community rules to depress national standards. However, the technique used in Article 100a(4) is quite distinct. Article 100a(4) is addressed to the capacity of states to opt out of the agreed Community norm, rather than to the development of the content of the Community norm.[21]

Article 100a(4) envisages circumstances in which free trade may yield to national standards which are pitched above the Community norm. In this sense Article 100a(4) should be categorized with the technique of minimum harmonization, although in its detail it offers less flexibility to the member state wishing to depart the

---

21. The only case dealing with Art. 100a(4) that has reached the European Court is Case C-41/93 *France v Commission* [1994] ECR I-1829, where the Court insisted on its narrow scope in annulling as inadequately reasoned a Commission Decision permitting Germany to apply stricter rules than laid down in an Art. 100a Directive.

agreed norm. Consumer protection is not explicitly mentioned in Article 100a(4), but Article 36, which *is* mentioned, refers to the protection of the health of humans. Accordingly, national measures concerned with consumer safety may be applied in derogation from a Community rule adopted under Article 100a, provided that the Article 100a(4) procedure is followed. However, there seems to be no scope for reliance on Article 100a(4) as a basis for the application of measures concerned with protection of the economic interests of consumers which go beyond a Community measure made under Article 100a.

Articles 100a(3) and (4) and, broader still, the technique of minimum harmonization are highly instructive in an understanding of the shaping of consumer policy and, indeed, of Community regulatory policy generally. The attraction of establishing common rules is initially strong, yet in a Community enjoying both functional and geographic expansion, a unidimensional insistence on harmonization as a tool of trade liberalization alone fails to take account of the range of interests which are intimately affected by market integration. Recognition that the adoption of a rigid, uniform and immutable Community norm is not the necessary and inevitable consequence of Community intervention in a particular field is highly significant. This issue is not new,[22] but the stakes are getting higher. It is neither politically feasible nor economically desirable to expect all fifteen member states to advance as a single bloc in all the sectors of economic activity now affected by EC policy. This trend away from the single Community rule carries the potential to cause the fragmentation of the Community market, yet it may be seen as a realistic attempt to accommodate diverse national tradition and consumer expectation within the process of integration.

Soft law and the completion of the internal market

Once the Community had set in train the project of completing the internal market by the end of 1992, which was given constitutional impetus by the entry into force of the SEA in 1987, initiatives in the field of consumer protection rapidly came to be

---

[22.] C.-D. Ehlermann, 'How Flexible is Community Law? An Unusual Approach to the Concept of "Two Speeds" ' 82 Michigan Law Rev 1274 (1984).

viewed within the framework of internal market strategy. This theme was taken up in the soft law expressions of consumer policy. Following the first and second Resolutions of 1975 and 1981, mentioned above, the third Council Resolution, of 23 June 1986, concerning the future orientation of the policy of the European Economic Community for the protection and promotion of consumer interests was expressed within the context of internal market policy.[23] The Council Resolution welcomed the Commission's paper of 23 June 1986, entitled 'A New Impetus for Consumer Protection Policy'.[24] In that paper, the Commission had reviewed progress. The Commission's view was that progress towards the realization of the objectives of the 1975 Resolution fell short of what had been expected. It was certainly true that if one measured the success of the programmes by the number of Directives adopted, then the progress was slow indeed. In the first ten years since 1975, a very small number of consumer-related measures had been adopted. Those which had been adopted lay primarily in the rather technical field of food labelling.

The Commission's paper identified four principal reasons for the relatively limited progress achieved: (1) economic recession diminishing willingness to fund initiatives; (2) the view that many consumer protection issues are properly matters for individual states, not the Community; (3) the requirement of unanimity in Council for the adoption of legislation under Articles 100 and 235 EC; (4) the practice of vertical harmonization, covering only a limited range of goods.

In the Commission's view, all these factors had combined to impede the passage of Community measures relevant to the protection of the consumer. In its review of this collection of obstacles, the Commission attempted to impose a positive outlook on the prevailing situation. It was in no mood to accept that these problems were decisive. The Commission rejected the idea that consumer protection should be a 'fair-weather' phenomenon and asserted that, because national consumer laws may affect market integration, they must accordingly be taken into account by Community policy makers. The Commission also took the opportunity in its paper to explain its future preoccupation with the more flexible 'new approach' to technical harmonization (Chapter 7). The Commission could not itself

23. OJ 1986 C167/1.   24. COM (85) 314.

address the impediment caused by the constitutional requirement of unanimity in Council, for that was part of the very structure of the Treaty, but, as already discussed, that issue was addressed in the SEA, particularly through the insertion of Article 100a.

The Commission proposed a new impetus in consumer protection policy, aiming at three main objectives: (1) products traded in the Community should conform to acceptable safety and health standards; (2) consumers must be able to benefit from the common market; (3) consumer interests should be taken more into account in other Community policies.

The Council Resolution, which welcomed the Commission's paper, was relatively brief. It stressed the objective of improving the ability of consumers to benefit from the Community's internal market. Moreover, it adopted a theme contained within the Commission's paper by linking the consumer interest with the notion of a 'People's Europe'. The Council Resolution called on the Commission to prepare proposals.

Perhaps the most striking overt change between the 1986 document, the third in the series, and the earlier programmes of 1975 and 1981 is the diminution in assertion of consumer 'rights'.[25] The discussion treated the consumer as the beneficiary of the process of market integration. Consumer choice, rather than consumer rights, emerged as the dominant theme.

In December 1986 the Council adopted a Resolution on the integration of consumer policy in the other common policies.[26] This readdressed the themes already set out in the Resolution of June 1986. It repeated the objective of taking greater account of consumers' interests in other Community policies. The Resolution is a response to a Commission communication under the title, 'Integration of Consumer Policy into other Common Policies', and, drafted in a rather general style, it encourages the Commission to pursue the matter.

The series of soft law declarations continued with a Council Resolution of November 1989 on future priorities for relaunching consumer protection policy.[27] In essence, this amounted to no more than a consolidation of pre-existing policy. It emphasized once again the link between consumer protection policy and the

---

[25.] N. Reich, 'Protection of Consumers' Economic Interests by the EC' 14 Sydney Law Rev 23 (1992).
[26.] OJ 1987 C3/1.   [27.] OJ 1989 C 294/1.

effective completion of the internal market. More generally, it referred to the consumer benefit which would accrue from the completion of the internal market. An Annex to the Resolution contained a list of priority areas, covering the integration of consumer protection policy into other common policies; improving consumer representation; promoting general safety of goods and services and better information on the quality of goods and services; encouraging member states to promote access to legal redress; and pursuing work on other specified initiatives.

In May 1990 the Commission initiated an adjustment in the pattern of its soft law strategy. It issued the first three-year action plan of consumer policy, to cover the period from 1990 to 1992.[28] Part A of the document offered a brief summary of 'Consolidation of Progress'. Part B provided a 'Three-Year Action Plan'. There were four main areas of focus within the plan, which were selected because of their contribution to building consumer confidence necessary to support the realization of the internal market. The four chosen areas were: consumer representation; consumer information; consumer safety; and consumer transactions.

This proved to be the last soft law instrument in the consumer field issued before the Treaty on European Union was agreed at Maastricht in December 1991.

The Treaty on European Union and consumer policy

The Treaty on European Union was agreed at Maastricht in December 1991 and signed there on 7 February 1992, but it could enter into force only when all the member states had ratified the Treaty. A combination of domestic difficulties in several states delayed this moment, but the Treaty eventually entered into force on 1 November 1993. It converted the former European Economic Community into the European Community.[29] This was largely a transformation of symbolic importance, which drew attention to broadening spheres of influence of the Community, beyond the economy as narrowly conceived.

28. COM (90) 98   29. Art. G.A.(i) TEU.

From the perspective of the consumer interest, the most striking change wrought by the Union Treaty was the inclusion in the Treaty, for the first time, of a separate Title devoted to consumer protection. The new Title XI: Consumer Protection comprises a new provision, Article 129a EC:

1. The Community shall contribute to the attainment of a high level of consumer protection through:

(a) measures adopted pursuant to Article 100a in the context of the completion of the internal market;

(b) specific action which supports and supplements the policy pursued by the member states to protect the health, safety and economic interests of consumers and to provide adequate information to consumers.

2. The Council, acting in accordance with the procedure referred to in Article 189b and after consulting the Economic and Social Committee, shall adopt the specific action referred to in paragraph 1(b).

3. Action adopted pursuant to paragraph 2 shall not prevent any member state from maintaining or introducing more stringent protective measures. Such measures must be compatible with this Treaty. The Commission shall be notified of them.

The elevation of consumer protection to the status of a Community common policy is confirmed by Article 3, as amended, which provides that '. . . the activities of the Community shall include . . . (o) a contribution to the attainment of a high level of health protection . . . (s) a contribution to the strengthening of consumer protection'.

Each of the paragraphs of Article 129a contains phrases, the effect of which is far from clear.

The first paragraph of Article 129a commits the Community to the attainment of a high level of protection, whereas Article 100a(3) committed only the Commission to that task. This seems to involve a firmer, more feasibly justiciable, obligation.

The reference to the adoption of 'specific action' in Article 129a(b) is puzzling. The phrase seems new to Community law. Presumably, 'specific action' embraces the full Article 189 list of available instruments, yet goes beyond that list. Presumably, the use of the full legislative procedure referred to in Article 129a(2) is appropriate only for binding legal acts (Regulations, Directives, Decisions) and not for mere soft law. However, these points remain to be authoritatively decided.

Nevertheless as a bare minimum, Article 129a provides a potential constitutional basis for the development of an EC strategy on consumer protection which is independent of harmonization policy in particular, and the process of market integration in general. Pre-Maastricht, the absence of a separate Title on consumer protection has acted as an unavoidable brake on the possibility of developing an autonomous body of laws in the area. Article 129a offers the prospect for a consumer policy no longer subordinate to the dictates of internal market policy.

However, the removal of any explicit objection to the Community's consitutional power to act in the field does not in any way remove the difficulty in assembling sufficient political support for individual proposals among the member states. A qualified majority is more readily achieved in Council than unanimity, yet even QMV requires a significant majority of member states to subscribe to an initiative. The problems are deepened by the obscurity of the relationship between Article 3b, the subsidiarity principle, and Article 129a. This, indeed, is an observation that can be directed at the impact of the subsidiarity principle on all of the Community's common policies. Subsidiarity is explored further below.

An institutional consideration hints at justifiable optimism that consumer policy may have come of age with its 'constitutionalization' in the Treaty amended at Maastricht. In 1995, for the first time, a separate Consumer Policy Directorate-General was established within the Commission. The Commission first granted institutional recognition to its functions with regard to the consumer in 1968, when it established an administrative unit as part of the Competition Policy Directorate-General. Since then, responsibility for consumer policy in the Commission has drifted among different entities. Between 1981 and 1989 it was part of a rather loosely conceived Directorate-General XI, alongside Environmental and Nuclear Affairs. From 1989 consumer policy was driven by a Consumer Policy Service within the Commission, which lacked the status of a Directorate-General. Consumer policy suffered from a low budget and vulnerability to the policy concerns of more powerful Directorates-General, most notably those dealing with agriculture and the internal market. The transformation of the Consumer Policy Service into a Directorate-General (DG XXIV, headed by Emma Bonino) in March 1995 does not necessarily remedy such weaknesses, but it may be viewed as a step up for consumer policy which may be advanced further over time.

The first occasion on which Article 129a EC was used as a base for Community action was in the field of product safety (Chapter 7). The Community has a policy, dating from 1981, on collecting statistical information about causes of injury with a view to regulating in areas shown to present particular risks to consumers.[30] This became the European Home and Leisure Accident Surveillance System (EHLASS) in 1986, as a result of a Council Decision based on Article 235, which was stated to form part of the promotion of a consumer protection policy.[31] The system of information on home and leisure accidents is now found in Decision 3092/94.[32] This is a decision of the Parliament and the Council made on the basis of Article 129a(2) EC and therefore in accordance with the Article 189b legislative procedure. Its objective is to collect data on home and leisure accidents with a view to promoting accident prevention, improving the safety of consumer products and informing and educating consumers so that they make better use of products. It covers the period from 1994 to 1997.

The relationship of Article 129a with other Treaty provisions

Articles 129a(1)(b) and 129a(2) establish a competence to act in the field of consumer protection which is independent of the process of legislating to complete the internal market under Article 100a, the subject of separate reference in Article 129a(1)(a). Although one might regard this as an important advance in the status of autonomous consumer policy making, the exercise of this legislative competence may lead to difficulties in establishing a demarcation between Articles 129a(2) and 100a. It may be difficult to determine when a legislative initiative touching on consumer protection is properly viewed as a

---

30. Decision 81/623/EEC OJ 1981 L229/1.
31. Decision 86/138/EEC OJ 1986 L109/23. Subsequently amended and extended, OJ 1990 L296/64, OJ 1993 L319/40.
32. OJ 1994 L331/1, amended by Dec. 95/184 OJ 1995 L120/36 to take account of the accession of Austria, Finland and Sweden in 1995.

contribution to internal market policy or as a contribution to the objectives indicated in Articles 129a(1)(b). Not infrequently, measures will perform both functions. The European Court may be called on to determine the correct base for a measure relevant to both consumer protection and the completion of the internal market. The Court has insisted, in litigation relevant to other demarcations, that the choice must be made according to objective factors amenable to judicial review.[33] It has been forced to carry out such a review function in the choice between Article 100a and Article 130s (Environmental Policy),[34] which is perhaps the closest analogy to the choice that would have to be made between Article 100a and Article 129a. It is, regrettably, difficult to draw clear principles from the Court's rulings on choice of legal base.[35] The need to choose a primary purpose for measures which, in a complex economy, have several impacts, is troubling. Although the Court is correct to deprive the political institutions of discretion to make tactical selections of legal base to suit their own interest, it has taken to itself a difficult task of adjudication. The issue of achieving this demarcation remains to be resolved in the future elaboration of Community consumer policy after the coming into force of the Treaty on European Union.

Article 129a(3) follows the minimum harmonization formula. As mentioned above, this is more permissive of national action than Article 100a(4), yet reflective of the same broad notion that underlies Article 100a(4) – that in the field of consumer protection laws the Community has moved away from an expectation that Community rules will operate as inflexible, uniform norms which pre-empt the opportunity for independent regulatory innovation by member states. However, the fact that Article 100a(4) is narrower than Article 129a(3) is a reason why there is practical significance in making the demarcation between Articles 100a and 129a, even though both provisions employ the same Article 189b legislative procedure.

---

33. For example, Case 45/86 *Commission v Council* [1987] ECR 1493; Case 68/86 *United Kingdom v Council* [1988] ECR 855.
34. Case C-300/89 *Commission v Council* [1991] ECR I-2867, preferring Art. 100a; Case C-155/91 *Commission v Council* judgment of 17 March 1993, preferring Art. 130s.
35. N. Emiliou, 'Opening Pandora's Box: The Legal Basis of Community Measures before the Court of Justice' 19 ELRev 488 (1994).

Soft law post-Maastricht

The Council Resolution of 29 June 1992 on future priorities for the development of consumer protection policy was passed at a time when prospects for the entry into force of the Treaty on European Union hung in the balance. The Resolution was important as a confirmation of the principles of the consumer protection policy, notwithstanding the sudden doubts which surrounded the future of the Treaty which envisaged an independent consumer protection Title. The Resolution was also an invitation to the Commission to develop the policy further.

An Annex to the Resolution identified six priority areas. These were integration into other common policies of the policy of consumer protection and promotion of consumers' interests; consumer information and education; legal redress; safety and health; representation of consumers; and economic interests.

The Commission proceeded to adopt its second three-year action plan, for 1993–95 in July 1993.[36] The sub-title of the plan, 'Placing the single market at the service of European consumers', demonstrates the post-1992 focus of the Commission's thinking. The plan is also adopted in the light of the new commitment to consumer protection enshrined in the Treaty on European Union, even though at the time of the plan's publication, the Treaty had not yet entered into force, and would not enter into force until 1 November 1993.

The second three-year plan has two main components: first, 'Consolidation of Community legislation in favour of consumers'; second, 'Selective priorities for raising the level of consumer protection'.

Under the first heading, 'Consolidation of Community legislation in favour of consumers', there are three subsections. The first covers the first three-year action plan. It surveys the instruments adopted in 1990–92 and the Commission proposals not yet adopted by the Council. The second subsection covers effective application of Community consumer law. The Commission pledges to maintain vigilance in checking implementation of Community acts at national level. The third subsection discusses new action. The Commission will continue to make such proposals as appear to it to be necessary, 'taking into account the principle of subsidiarity'.

36. COM (93) 378.

Under the second heading, 'Selective priorities for raising the level of consumer protection', there are five sub-headings:

(1) *Strengthening consumer information.* The Commission regards this as a key element in overcoming consumer uncertainty about the operation of the internal market. The improvement of information provision as a means of achieving market transparency is to be realized through legislative action and other more general support for information provision, such as Commission support for price surveys and comparative testing. The development of a network of transfrontier consumer information centres, which is already under way, is also heralded as an important contribution to consumer information. This is examined in Chapter 8 of this book.

(2) *Enhancing and expanding concertation.* The Commission is committed to deepening the process whereby consumer views are made known to the Commission.

(3) *Furthering access to justice and the settlement of disputes.* Access to justice, a key issue in consumer protection generally, becomes acutely important in transfrontier situations. The Commission promised a Green Paper on the subject, which appeared later in 1993. It is discussed in Chapter 8 of this book.

(4) *Adapting financial services to consumer needs.* Some such developments, both formal and informal, are examined in Chapter 3 of this book.

(5) *Preparing new stages.*

The plan concludes by declaring a commitment to concentrate on areas which are crucial for consumer confidence in the internal market. These include consumer information, access to justice, and consumer health and safety. The objective of integrating consumer policy in other common policies also remains an integral part of the policy.

The third three-year action plan was published by the Commission in October 1995 and covers the period 1996–98.[37] The plan discusses the need to tie up the loose ends of the internal market, but the message of the document is that

[37.] COM (95) 519.

consumer policy should now look beyond the 1992 project. It asserts that Article 129a requires the Community to deal with a broad sweep of consumer issues, not simply those connected with internal market policy. The plan is notable for a relative dearth of concrete legislative proposals. Ten priorities for action are picked out. These relate to:

(1) improving the education and information of consumers;
(2) devoting continued attention to ensuring that consumers' interests are taken fully into account in the internal market;
(3) the consumer aspect of financial services;
(4) protecting consumer interests in the supply of essential services of public utility;
(5) measures to enable consumers to benefit from opportunities presented by the Information Society;
(6) measures to improve consumer confidence in foodstuffs;
(7) encouraging a practical approach to sustainable consumption;[38]
(8) strengthening and increasing consumer representation;
(9) assisting Central and Eastern European countries to develop consumer policies;
(10) consumer policy considerations in developing countries.

Subsidiarity and consumer policy

Modern moods of scepticism about the desirable intensity of Community regulation, mentioned at the start of this chapter, have tended to be debated in the context of the subsidiarity principle, inserted into the EC Treaty by the Treaty on European Union. Article 3b, the principle of subsidiarity, provides that:

> The Community shall act within the limits of the powers conferred upon it by this Treaty and of the objectives assigned to it therein.
>
> In areas which do not fall within its exclusive competence, the Community shall take action, in accordance with the principle of subsidiarity, only if and in so far as the objectives of the proposed action cannot be sufficiently achieved by the member states and

---

38. Cf. C. Kye. 'Environmental Law and the Consumer in the EU' 7 Journal of Environmental Law 31 (1995).

can therefore, by reason of the scale or effects of the proposed action, be better achieved by the Community.

Any action by the Community shall not go beyond what is necessary to achieve the objectives of this Treaty.

Article 3b is, in many ways, no more than a series of implied questions. It raises questions about the scope of Community competence which relate both to the absolute scope of Community competence and to the scope of Community competence relative to that of the member states. It also asks questions about the relationship between different areas of Community competence, involving questions of choosing the correct Treaty base for proposed legislation and the institutional implications of such a choice. In all these respects, the EC Treaty's lack of a specific allocation of competences, demarcated between Community and states (in contrast to, for example, the German Basic Law), coupled to the past tendency of the EC's legislative and judicial institutions to preside over an outward drift in EC competence (with a corresponding diminution in the scope of exclusive national competence) has stimulated a harder look at the motivations for action in the Community.

Contrary to some politicians' views, the principle of subsidiarity is improperly perceived simply as a means of reducing the scope of Community obligations. Its focus is efficient administration. Sir Leon Brittan has helpfully described it as a method for identifying the 'best level' for regulatory activity in the Community.[39] This rendition is important and, it is submitted, helpful, because it brings out the point that subsidiarity is not based on preconceptions about centralization or decentralization. Instead, it is a matter of *efficiency* – problematic though such a test will doubtless prove to be in its practical application, by politicians and/or by judges.

Consumer policy has been overtly affected by perceptions based on subsidiarity. For example, the principle has formed the basis for the argument that the implementation of Community policy initiatives should be devolved more readily to national and local level, thereby reducing the administrative capacity of the Community institutions. This seems to have been conceded by the

[39] Sir Leon Brittan, 'Institutional Development of the EC' Public Law 567 (1992).

31

Commission, even before Maastricht. In the consumer policy action plan 1990–92,[40] the Commission declared, under the heading 'Subsidiarity Principle', that:

> Practical consumer policy must be effectively managed in the member states on an ongoing basis with the management and control of safety, information and redress being adapted in each instance to local needs. It would be unrealistic to undertake such tasks continuously at a Community level.

None the less, some of the clamour about subsidiarity in the consumer field has been plainly directed at curtailment of Community activity. Reacting to this tendency, Leigh Gibson has observed acutely that:

> There has been particular resistance to EC involvement in action to improve consumer access to justice and redress for disputes concerning cross-border purchases of defective goods and services. What is significant is the absence of any other initiatives to tackle this issue outside of the Community framework. Subsidiarity cloaks a failure to act with the respectability of a principled stand. Member states have interpreted it as a concise formula for inaction at any level rather than as a vehicle for establishing the appropriate level for effective action.[41]

In similar vein, the EC's Economic and Social Committee has declared that subsidiarity 'might be abused and might jeopardise any EC initiatives whose specific aim is to promote consumers' interests',[42] emphasizing the risk that the integrated market will go underregulated if initiatives are blocked.

However, it appears that some member states are prepared to see subsidiarity used as a device for blocking Community action. For example, it is known that the German government issued a list in which it proposed a radical reduction in Community measures touching on consumer policy,[43] although Directive 93/13 on Unfair Terms in Consumer Contracts was adopted subsequently (Chapter 4), so one should not overestimate the depth of German intransigence. One might guess that the UK

40. COM (90) 98.
41. L. Gibson, 'Subsidiarity: the Implications for Consumer Policy' 16 JCP 323 (1993).
42. OJ 1993 C19/22.
43. Printed in *Verbraucher und Recht* 1/1993.

government would have sympathy for the German attitude. In April 1993 the House of Commons European Standing Committee, discussing the proposed Distant Selling Directive (Chapter 3), was told by the minister that one member state, which he was unprepared to name on grounds of confidentiality, had proposed the abandonment of the Directive on the basis that it violated the subsidiarity principle.[44] It would not be incautious to guess that Germany was the unnamed state in question, and the proposal remains unadopted. This glimpse of subsidiarity in action might induce forgivable scepticism about claims that subsidiarity can serve as an element in democratization of the Community. Not only was the substance of the Council debate drawn from subsidiarity kept secret, so too was the very identity of the state which had raised the point! In any event, such shreds of evidence indicate that subsidiarity is part of the context in which EC consumer policy is debated.

At the meeting of the European Council in Edinburgh in December 1992, emphasis was placed on subsidiarity as a means for persuading the states then wavering (for different reasons) over ratifying the Treaty on European Union that the Community was committed to showing due respect for national traditions. The European Council agreed an overall approach to the application of the subsidiarity principle, which was annexed to the conclusions of the Presidency. It invited the Council to seek an inter-institutional agreement between the European Parliament, the Council and the Commission on the effective application of Article 3b by all institutions. A text was agreed in 1993. In addition, a report submitted to the European Council by Jacques Delors, the President of the Commission, was annexed. This report contained the first fruits of the Commission's review of existing and proposed legislation in the light of the subsidiarity principle. The Commission's report declared that it had withdrawn three proposals for Directives in the light of the demands of the principle of subsidiarity. One of these impinged on consumer policy, a Directive dealing with compulsory indication of nutritional value on the packaging of foodstuffs. Consideration was being given to withdrawing several further proposals. A third group of proposals was singled out because of the inclusion of excessive detail. These Directives were to be

44. H.C. EC Standing Committee B, 28 April 1993.

revised and drafted in a more general style. This batch included proposals relating to the liability of suppliers of services (Chapter 5) and comparative advertising (Chapter 6).

The overall approach to the application by the Council of the subsidiarity principle, annexed to the conclusions of the Presidency, draws from the third paragraph of Article 3b the need to consider setting minimum standards only, where it is necessary to set standards at Community level. This is to apply beyond areas of the Treaty which make specific reference to minimum standards. It will apply in other areas 'where this would not conflict with the objectives of the proposed measure or with the Treaty'. As discussed above, the use of minimum standards is well established in the consumer law field. The same paper also explicitly states that 'Other things being equal, directives should be preferred to regulations and framework directives to detailed measures', and that 'Non-binding measures such as recommendations should be preferred where appropriate. Consideration should also be given where appropriate to the use of voluntary codes of conduct'. EC consumer policy reflects such trends. It is characterized by a network of non-binding instruments.

The Commission made three commitments with regard to the application of the subsidiarity principle in a further report to the European Council in Brussels in December 1993. In relation to consumer policy, it would justify all new legislative proposals with reference to Article 3b; withdraw or revise certain pending proposals; and continue work on the proposals in the field of liability of suppliers of services and comparative advertising. In this report, the Commission observed that 'Subsidiarity cannot be reduced to a set of procedural rules; it is primarily a state of mind'. This may be true, but different states of mind exist at different times in different Community institutions and different member states!

The Commission issued its first annual report on the subsidiarity principle in November 1994.[45] The Commission declared that its objective was to take fewer initiatives, but to target those taken more effectively. Naturally, planning a reduction in legislative output was facilitated by the ending of the period of intense activity connected with the 1992 project. The Commission stated an intention to launch initiatives only after review from the perspective of subsidiarity and proportionality.

45. COM (94) 533.

The process of withdrawal and revision, begun at Edinburgh, was to continue.

The Commission commented that 'one cannot help observing that principle and practice are often far apart with member states meeting within the Council often adopting positions on individual cases at variance with their respect in principle for Article 3b'. This wry remark confirms that the debate between the Community institutions and the member states about the appropriate intensity of Community consumer policy making, both in absolute terms and relative to state action in the field, has been sharpened, and by no means resolved, by the language of subsidiarity.

CHAPTER TWO

Negative law and market integration

Market integration and consumer choice

The transformation of relatively small-scale national markets into a large single Community market will stimulate competition and induce producers to achieve maximum efficiency in order to protect, and *a fortiori* to expand, their market share. As a matter of economic theory, this intensification of competition should serve the consumer by increasing the available choice of goods and services, thereby inducing improvements in their quality and reduction in their price.

The law is an instrument in this process. Article 30 EC serves to eliminate national measures that partition product markets. Article 59 EC fulfils the same function in the market for services. Removal of barriers to cross-border trade in goods and services stimulates competition and enhances consumer choice. The Treaty competition rules, too, have as one objective the prevention of practices that cause fragmentation of the market along national lines. In this sense, the law of market integration is itself a form of (indirect) consumer policy. The achievement of a common market will benefit the consumer, and accordingly the legal prohibition of national measures and practices that impede trade across borders is in the consumer interest. These prohibitions are frequently grouped together as 'negative law': law that forbids action hostile to the interpenetration of national markets.

Consumer choice is an occasional explicit visitor to the Court's judgments. The Court has declared that the legislation of a member state must not 'crystallize given consumer habits so as to consolidate an advantage acquired by national industries concerned to comply with them'. The Court has made this observation in the context of both fiscal rules which favour typical national products[1] and technical rules which exert a similar protectionist effect.[2] The first case involved the British system of taxing alcoholic beverages, which favoured beer over wine and which, accordingly, protected the typical domestic product, beer, from competition from a typically imported product, wine. The second case involved German rules which were based on assumptions about beer-making techniques typical in Germany but not the norm elsewhere, which resulted in the German beer market being closed off to brewers based in other states using different recipes. In neither case did the European Court's ruling prevent producers adopting favoured techniques. Rather, the Court was concerned to prevent the public authorities making choices on behalf of consumers. The elimination of the national rule permitted consumers to make their own choice without the distorting influence of state intervention.

A case dealing with the services sector, *Commission v France*,[3] provides a simple illustration of the Court's approach. French rules obliged tourist guides to obtain a licence. This rule exerted a restrictive effect on the ability of tourist guides from outside France to accompany groups who wished to tour France. The Court did not deny the legitimacy of the objective of ensuring proper cultural and artistic appreciation of the host country, but found the rules in question disproportionately restrictive. As the Court observed, the French rules would be likely to have the effect that visiting groups would be denied the opportunity to be guided by someone 'who is familiar with their language, their interests and their specific expectations'. The decision serves to enhance market integration and consumer choice.

Deregulating the market by abolishing state intervention incompatible with Articles 30 and 59 is accompanied by the use of the Treaty competition rules to control anti-competitive and anti-integrative practices in the private sector. The Court has on occasion explicitly referred to the consumer interest in securing free competition in accordance with Article 85. In *Zuchner v Bayerische Vereinsbank AG*[4] the Court ruled that Article 85 may

---

[1.] Art. 95 EC: Case 170/178 *Commission v United Kingdom* [1980] ECR 417.
[2.] Case 178/84 *Commission v Germany* [1987] ECR 1227.
[3.] Case C-154/89 [1991] ECR 1-659.   [4.] Case 172/80 [1981] ECR 2021.

apply where firms have abandoned their independence in favour of unlawful collusion which suppresses competition, '... thus depriving their customers of any genuine opportunity to take advantage of services on more favourable terms which would be offered to them under normal conditions of competition'. *Cooperatieve vereniging Suiker Unie UA and others v Commission*[5] concerned practices which led to the isolation of national markets from cross-border competition. The Court found that such arrangements were 'to the detriment of effective freedom of movement of the products in the common market and of the freedom of consumers to choose their suppliers'. For agreements that fall within Article 85(1), exemption is available under Article 85(3) only on condition that it, inter alia, 'contributes to improving the production of goods or to promoting technical or economic progress, while allowing consumers a fair share of the resulting benefit ...'. This is one of the few explicit references to the consumer in the Treaty, although its impact as a tool of consumer policy is diluted, first, by the point that 'consumer' in this context covers any user of the item, not simply the end user[6] and, second, by the Commission's readiness to assume that, provided an agreement promotes efficient commercial structures and provided a sufficient level of competition endures, then the consumer will benefit in consequence.[7]

Article 86 has a role to play in sustaining consumer choice. Included in the list of illustrative abuses of a dominant position in Article 86 is 'limiting production, markets or technical development to the prejudice of consumers ...'. This may be used to require a dominant firm to respond to consumer demand. The Commission's insistence that television companies which printed separate guides to future programmes using copyright over the listings to prevent the publication of a single, integrated guide had breached Article 86 was upheld by the European Court, on appeal from the decision of the Court of First Instance. The Court observed that the companies, the sole sources of the raw material needed for compiling a weekly guide, had unjustifiably

---

5. Cases 40–48, 50, 54–56, 111, 113 & 114/73 [1975] ECR 1663.
6. This is better reflected in the French text, which refers to 'utilisateur', rather than 'consommateur'.
7. A. Evans, 'European Competition Law and Consumers: the Article 85(3) Exemption' ECLR 425 (1981).

blocked the appearance of a new product for which a potential consumer demand existed.[8]

Towards consumer rights

The Court has developed EC trade law into a charter of consumer *choice*. The consumer is able to benefit from the fruits of market integration by buying goods and services imported by traders from other member states while resident in his or her home state. This may be taken further, into the realms of active consumer rights. In *GB-INNO-BM v Confederation du Commerce Luxembourgeois (CCL)*[9] the Court declared that:

> Free movement of goods concerns not only traders but also individuals. It requires, particularly in frontier areas, that consumers resident in one Member State may travel freely to the territory of another Member State to shop under the same conditions as the local population.

The Court determined in *Luisi and Carbone v Ministero del Tesero*[10] that 'tourists, persons receiving medical treatment and persons travelling for the purpose of education or business' are to be regarded as recipients of services who enjoy the right of free movement under Article 59. As already foreshadowed by Article 1(1)(b) of Directive 73/148,[11] which confers a right of free movement and residence on those wishing to migrate in order to receive services, the consumer as an economically active migrant enjoys rights of entry, residence and non-discrimination. The Court has interpreted the right to non-discriminatory treatment within the scope of the Treaty broadly. In *Cowan v Le Tresor Public*[12] the European Court found that a tourist, as a recipient of services, was entitled to compensation for criminally inflicted injuries on the same terms as those applicable to nationals of the host state. This was the product of the combined application of Article 59, the free movement of services, and Article 6, the rule against nationality discrimination within the scope of application

---

8. Cases C-241/91 P, C-242/91 P *RTE and ITP v Commission* [1995] ECR II-801.
9. Case C-362/88 [1990] ECR I-667.
10. Cases 286/82 & 26/83 [1984] ECR 377.
11. OJ 1973 L172/14. 12. Case 186/87 [1989] ECR 195.

of the Treaty. The Court's decision in *Cowan* envisages an extended notion of the need to ensure equal access to social benefits as part of the policy of securing the elimination of impediments to migration.

The notion of consumer rights is bolstered by the post-1992 legislative adjustments which have permitted consumers (though not commercial operators) to buy goods duty-paid in another member state and return with them for private consumption without hindrance by the home state.

It remains questionable how far beyond equal treatment with host state nationals and open access to markets of other states it is necessary for the law to reach in order to induce consumers actively to explore the advantages of the internal market. The question: to what extent is 'positive' Community legislation required in support of 'negative' law? is a key question in the general development of Community consumer policy, and the evolution of a framework of consumer protection law at Community level is traced through the remaining chapters of this book.

It is more normal in the field of 'negative law' for the examination of the compatibility of national rules which obstruct trade with substantive Community law to be undertaken without explicit reference to the position of the consumer. For all the hints of consumer as right-holder in the law of the internal market, the consumer is normally cast merely as the passive beneficiary of cross-border commercial activity. Indeed, the bold assertion of consumer rights in *GB-INNO* appears in a ruling delivered in the context of a Belgian trader's successful reliance on Article 30 to set aside a Luxembourg rule obstructive of a cross-border commercial strategy.

Competing notions of the consumer interest

National rules which obstruct cross-border trade are enforceable only where they serve an interest of sufficient importance to override the principle of free movement and where they are apt and proportionate to achieve that objective. One justification for obstructive national rules recognized under Community law is the protection of the consumer. There are a number of cases under both Articles 30 and 59 which pit the consumer interest in integration, served by eliminating trade-restrictive national laws, against the consumer interest in protection, which dictates the maintenance of national regulations. National consumer protection law may come into collision with Community law of market integration, which is itself designed to advance the consumer interest. These cases force the Court to develop its own notion of the consumer interest in defining the scope of application of Community trade law. This is in accordance with one of this book's themes: that the EC institutions, in this instance the Court, have been forced by the growth of EC law and policy to develop an approach to the consumer interest despite the absence in the Treaty pre-Maastricht of any explicit place for consumer policy. That is to say, the simple divide between the Community's interest in securing market integration and the states' responsibility to citizens to select appropriate levels of social and economic regulation breaks down as the deepening process of integration calls into question national measures that may initially appear remote from cross-border trade.

This is an especially intriguing inquiry because it involves the Court making an examination of two competing conceptions of the consumer interest. Negative law is based on assumptions about the advantages of cross-border trade as a means of improving the functioning of the economy to the benefit of the consumer. Accordingly, national measures that impair product and service market integration are treated with suspicion. But some such national measures will themselves reflect domestic concern to protect the consumer from perceived failings of the market system. This is the clash of competing consumer interests: the Community-driven notion of free trade, versus the national choice about protection. Quite apart from positive regulation of the market in the consumer interest, agreed by the political institutions of the Community, the Court becomes a participant in the debate about the place of the consumer in a market economy where the application of negative law forces it to confront the validity of national choices about consumer protection that confine consumer choice.[13]

---

13. S. Weatherill, 'The Evolution of European Consumer Law and Policy: from well-informed consumer to confident consumer' in H.-W. Micklitz (ed.) *Rechtseinheit oder Rechtsvielfalt in Europa?* (Baden-Baden, Nomos, 1996).

Articles 30–36: the basic pattern of the law of the free movement of goods

Article 30 covers 'all trading rules enacted by member states which are capable of hindering, directly or indirectly, actually or potentially, intra-Community trade'.[14] This is the 'Dassonville' formula, recently narrowed in *Keck and Mithouard*[15] in which the Court, concerned to refocus Article 30 on to the elimination of market-partitioning measures, not simply measures which affect commerce generally, ruled that there is no actual or potential, direct or indirect, barrier to inter-state trade where national laws limit or prohibit certain selling arrangements, provided those laws apply to all traders active on the national territory and provided that they affect in the same way in law and in fact the marketing of national products and those originating in other member states.

Applying this broad definition, a ban or restriction on the marketing of a product is in principle capable of being caught by Article 30 where it affects intra-Community trade. More subtly, rules governing product composition are similarly capable of being caught by Article 30 where they impede the access to the market of goods made elsewhere according to different regulatory specifications.

Justification for obstructive rules under the relevant Chapter of the Treaty is available only under Article 36, which provides that 'The provisions of Articles 30 to 34 shall not preclude prohibitions or restrictions on imports, exports or goods in transit justified on grounds of . . . (inter alia) the protection of health and life of humans, animals or plants'. There is no explicit reference to the consumer in Article 36, but the notion of the protection of the health and life of humans is capable of covering the protection of the physical integrity of the consumer. Accordingly, national rules designed to secure health and safety may be enforced notwithstanding any impediment to integration,

---

[14.] Case 8/74 *Procureur du Roi v Dassonville* [1974] ECR 837. See S. Weatherill and P. Beaumont, *EC Law* (London, Penguin Books, 2nd edn, 1995), chs 15–17.

[15.] Cases C-267 & 268/91 *Keck and Mithouard*, judgment of 24 November 1993. See comment by L. Gormley in 'Reasoning Renounced? The remarkable judgment in Keck and Mithouard' European Business Law Rev 63 (1994). More broadly, on the Court's recent policy in this and related areas, see N. Reich, 'The November Revolution of the European Court of Justice: Keck, Meng and Audi Revisited' 31 CMLRev 459 (1994).

provided the conditions under Article 36 are satisfied. Justification under Article 36 encompasses the compatibility with Community law of both the end in view and the means chosen to achieve that end. This is inherent in the second sentence of Article 36, which declares that 'such prohibitions or restrictions shall not, however, constitute a means of arbitrary discrimination or a disguised restriction on trade between member states'. Accordingly, it is incumbent on the member state to show that the national measure adopted is apt to achieve the end in view and the least restrictive of trade necessary to achieve that end.

The Court is not prepared simply to accept at face value member state submissions that national measures are required to defend domestic health standards. In some cases the Court has demonstrated vigorous scepticism about an alleged threat to health. In *Commission v United Kingdom*[16] the UK sought to demonstrate that its restrictions on the import of poultry were justified in the light of the need to tackle the spread of Newcastle disease. The Court remarked on the haste with which the measures had been introduced in the approach to Christmas 1981, at a time when British turkey breeders were appealing for protection. There was scant evidence of a seriously considered health policy and the UK, acting in breach of Article 30 by obstructing imports, was unable to seek refuge in Article 36. In such circumstances the Court is, in effect, identifying national measures as devious protectionism in favour of home producers. Such a ruling, prohibiting national measures, asserts consumer choice through market integration.

However, Article 30 is not a charter for irresistible deregulation. States may permissibly protect domestic consumers even where this impedes integration. This is possible even where scientific evidence advanced to show a health risk posed by the product subject to control is equivocal. For example, in *Eyssen*[17] Dutch rules banning the use of nisin, a preservative, in processed cheese were presented as measures of health protection, yet other states were prepared to allow the use of nisin, adopting a different view of inconclusive scientific evidence about the safety of the substance. The Court held that a state may take precautions to protect its consumers against health risks in accordance with Article 36 where there is genuine scientific doubt

16. Case 40/82 [1982] ECR 2793.   17. Case 53/80 [1981] ECR 4091.

about the safety of the product. Community law does not depress national standards of protection to the lowest common denominator prevailing among the member states. The same perception of the limits to integration through negative law may be observed in *Aragonesa de Publicidad Exterior SA v Departamento de Sanidad y Seguridad Social de la Generalitat de Cataluna*,[18] where the Court found that measures that restricted the advertising of alcoholic drink above a certain threshold strength might impede market integration,[19] but that such intervention in the market might be accepted as part of a seriously considered health policy – even where other member states were content with more permissive regimes. So consumer choice is not the inevitable result of the impact of EC negative law; regulation by the public authorities remains permitted even where it obstructs cross-border trade, provided both ends and means are capable of justification against the standards recognized by Community law.

The 'Cassis de Dijon' principle

National measures which are designed to protect the economic interests of the consumer, yet which impede trade – such as rules against deceptive marketing practices or misleading product description, or rules encouraging or requiring the provision of information to consumers – seem to fall beyond the scope of Article 36. However, provided they are origin-neutral, such rules are capable of being defended, despite their restrictive effect on trade. The assessment of the compatibility of such national measures with Article 30 takes place against the background of one of the Court's most remarkable creations, the 'Cassis de Dijon' line of authority. This applies where disparity between technical standards in different member states relating to composition and – more extensively still – relating to marketing,

---

18. (*APESA v DSSC*) Cases C-1, C-176/90 [1991] ECR I-4151.
19. Although, post-*Keck and Mithouard* (above), an importer would have to show, loosely, how the rule affected cross-border commercial strategy (e.g. by preventing an integrated advertising plan) and not merely commercial freedom. Only then would the state be called on to justify its rules.

is shown to be capable of impeding trade by affecting imported goods more heavily in fact than home produced goods.

In the case itself[20] French blackcurrant liqueur could not be sold in Germany because it fell below the minimum alcohol requirement for such goods under German law. There was no question of discrimination on the face of the measure; it applied to all such products, wherever they were made. But, in practice, a product made in another state, where different technical specifications prevailed, could not gain access to the German market without modification. German products, by contrast, would naturally conform to their domestic regulatory system and would obtain an inevitable competitive advantage in Germany. Out-of-state producers would be unable to devise an integrated strategy for the whole EC market. German consumers would be denied the opportunity to choose products made according to different traditions. Short of harmonization of laws, the market would remain fragmented along national lines. This prospect prompted the Court to draw together and to refine its case law and to devise a formula which has proved an enduring basis for assessing the lawfulness of trade barriers that arise in consequence on diversity between national rules:

> Obstacles to movement in the Community resulting from disparities between the national laws in question must be accepted in so far as those provisions may be recognized as being necessary in order to satisfy mandatory requirements relating in particular to the effectiveness of fiscal supervision, the protection of public health, the fairness of commercial transactions and the defence of the consumer.

The same formula has been increasingly applied by the Court to Article 59, where similar economic issues arise and where the Court has accordingly developed a similar legal formula involving an assessment of the balance between the consumer interest in market integration, which would follow from the abolition of the national rule and the consumer interest in protection at national level at the expense of integration.

---

20. Case 120/78 *Rewe Zentrale v Bundesmonopolverwaltung für Branntwein* [1979] ECR 649 ('Cassis de Dijon').

Cassis de Dijon: institutional implications

The Court's moulding of Article 30 in this fashion has significant institutional consequences. Prohibiting a national rule contributes to free trade without the need for the Community to adopt legislation in the area. This has the gratifying consequence that diversity persists. Mutual recognition of diverse national traditions secures wider choice. This consequence of negative law has been termed 'negative harmonization'. Free trade is brought about by removing obstructive national rules. It is a fundamental aspect of the deregulatory impulse that pervades the law of market integration. A range of national rules that act as preconditions to market access are, if shown to be unjustified interference with the market, replaced by no precondition at all. Only where national rules are lawful, because they protect an interest of sufficient weight to override the law of market integration, is a positive response required in order to liberalize the market. This is 'positive law': harmonization – the adoption of common Community rules which replace divergent national rules in the field. Harmonization is both deregulatory in effect and re-regulatory. Up to 15 national rules are replaced by one, established at Community level.[21]

The Cassis de Dijon line of jurisprudence has substantially reduced the Commission's workload in the area of harmonization. Article 30 may now be employed to defeat a great many national technical rules which, prior to Cassis de Dijon, seemed capable of partitioning the market until such time as harmonization legislation could be adopted. Freed of this vast burden, the Commission may now concentrate its harmonization work in the remaining areas where national rules act as lawful impediments to trade and where Community intervention is appropriate.[22] Moreover, the extension of the Article 30 prohibition and the consequent diminution in the scope of the legislative programme has attractions beyond the perspective of a reduction in the Commission's workload. By shifting the focus to the circulation of traditional national products and away from

---

21. The many nuances of harmonization policy, which depart from this simple model, are tracked throughout this book.
22. Commission Communication OJ 1980 C256/2; COM (85) 310, the 'White Paper' on the Completion of the Internal Market, para. 61 et seq.

the need to adopt common Community rules, the rise of the 'Europroduct' is stifled. The need to sacrifice distinct national regulatory philosophies is averted by this preference for negative over positive Community law.

The placing of the line between lawful and unlawful national measures is fundamentally important. The Court, in its Cassis de Dijon formula, claims for itself the sensitive function of judging the competing merits of integration and national regulation, a choice which is institutionally significant in its implications for the margin between judge-led negative harmonization and the need for positive harmonization by legislative act.

Cassis de Dijon: a critique

It has been suggested that the Court may prioritize integration over legitimate national initiatives of consumer protection, as part of an overenthusiastic pursuit of an integrative function that should more properly belong with the Community's legislature. This debate will be tracked in the Court's case law. In part, it depends on perceptions of the capacity of the consumer to look after him- or herself in the market. Among some commentators, there is a perceived risk that even legitimate initiatives of national consumer protection may be inhibited because of the oppressive effect of Community law, which creates a climate of uncertainty about the lawfulness of national initiatives. This could lead to a 'regulatory gap', in which national action is deterred, but no Community action occurs either. For some, this drives the de-regulatory impulse of Community law too far into the legitimate scope of market regulation. A further aspect to the regulatory gap may arise because of the notorious difficulty in achieving legislative action at Community level, even where the need for it is widely recognized. Slow progress at legislative level is frequently not attributable simply to disagreement about the need for a measure, but rather to disagreement about its technical details. Then again, it may be that even where Community rules are agreed, their enforcement in practice is less than rigorous. This too will weaken the protection of the consumer. It is impossible to provide objective, comprehensive verification of the criticism that Community law is liable to lead to a deregulated market in which the consumer is left exposed to practices from which protection should be afforded. However, this critical framework for analysis of the Court's role *per se* and its relationship with the place of legislation should be borne in mind by the reader.[23]

Cassis de Dijon: straightforward applications of the rise of consumer choice

Many cases decided under Articles 30 and 59 are rather straightforward and uncontroversial. It is hard to disagree with the view that the consumer is better served by being able to choose between liqueurs of differing alcoholic strengths rather than by being 'protected' from unexpectedly weak drinks (the situation in Cassis de Dijon itself). Choosing between differently packaged margarines is surely better than only being able to buy cube-shaped packs – a situation which, as the Court commented and as economic theorists would expect, led to Belgian consumers paying more for their margarine than consumers in neighbouring states.[24] Community law liberalizes the market for products and services, thereby expanding the consumer's choice.

The Court relies on the capacity of the consumer to process information and, on that basis, to make informed choices about available products and services as a basis for ruling against national measures that go so far as to suppress the appearance on the market of imported products and services. In the application of the proportionality principle, the Court has frequently held unlawful stricter measures which suppress products where information provision might have sufficed to achieve consumer protection. These are cases which demonstrate the principle that even where the *end* of consumer protection may provide a justification for a trade-restrictive measure, the *means* employed must be the least restrictive of trade available which are capable of meeting the end in view.

The principle emerges from the Cassis de Dijon ruling itself, where the Court swept aside the alleged need for a statutory

---

23. Cf. H.-C. Von Heydebrand und der Lasa, 'Free Movement of Foodstuffs, Consumer Protection and Food Standards in the European Community: Has the Court of Justice got it wrong?' 16 ELRev 391 (1991); A. McGee and S. Weatherill, 'The Evolution of the Single Market – Harmonisation or Liberalisation? 53 Modern Law Rev 578 (1990); M. van Empel, 'The 1992 Programme: Interaction between Legislator and Judiciary' [1992/2] LIEI 1 (1992).

24. Case 261/81 *Walter Rau v de Smedt* [1982] ECR 3961.

minimum alcohol content 'since it is a simple matter to ensure that suitable information is conveyed to the purchaser by requiring the display of an indication of origin and of the alcohol content on the packaging of products'. In the 'Beer Purity' case, *Commission v Germany*,[25] the Court explicitly identified the availability of consumer information as a regulatory device which is less restrictive of trade than mandatory composition requirements. The Court commented that even where beers are sold on draught, information may be provided 'on the casks or the beer taps'. This is an application of the proportionality principle which is familiar in EC trade law, and through it EC law indirectly encourages information disclosure as part of the process of market integration. The intended result is that the informed consumer is enabled then to exercise choice in accordance with his or her own (informed) preferences, rather than have that choice confined by governmental intervention. The transfer of decision making powers away from the public authorities to the consumer is the key to these rulings.

This is not to say that national measures requiring that items be labelled are themselves *necessarily* compatible with Community law. Mandatory origin marking is likely to violate Community law as a result of the hindrance to market interpenetration which flows from consequent consumer prejudice in favour of domestic goods.[26] Even where a labelling requirement relates to a product's qualities, rather than its origin, an impediment to market integration is caused by the obligation imposed on an out-of-state producer to modify production runs in order to conform to the labelling law of the target state. Where information relevant to a product's composition can be conveyed on a label in a way which is adequate to alert the consumer to the nature of the product, then a rule which forbids the marketing of the product is disproportionate and cannot be justified, but a state must still show a justification for the labelling requirement. The Court has observed that intervention will not be justified 'if the details given on the original label of the imported product have as their content information on the nature of the product and that content includes at least the same

25. Case 178/84 [1987] ECR 1227.
26. E.g. Case 207/83 *Commission v UK* [1985] ECR 1202 and, more nuanced, Case C-3/91 *Exportur SA v LOR SA* judgment of 10 November 1992.

information, and is just as capable of being understood by consumers in the importing state, as the description prescribed by the rules of that state'.[27]

It remains true that where protection cannot be achieved by information provision, measures of a more restrictive nature may be justified. Situations where there is a health risk provide obvious examples. The rulings in *Eyssen* and *APESA v DSSC*, discussed at p. 43 above, demonstrate how EC law does not require public authorities to retreat totally from the task of market regulation, provided they are able to show a sufficient justification for not leaving a matter to unfettered consumer choice. Community law in this area retains a notion of the consumer who is inadequately protected by the free market and for whom even mandatory information disclosure is inadequate.

The Court's Cassis de Dijon formula involves a judicial assessment of national regulatory measures that obstruct trade which is informed by the ills of protectionism, yet which reflects in the mandatory requirements an appreciation of the role of national protective measures.

The ruling in *Drei Glocken v USL Centro-Sud*

A classic illustration of the grey areas that lie between lawful and unlawful national rules is provided by *Drei Glocken v USL Centro-Sud*.[28] Italian rules required the use of durum wheat alone in the manufacture of pasta products. Such rules had the effect of excluding pasta made according to different recipes and using different types of wheat in other member states. This was a classic Cassis de Dijon case of market fragmentation caused by disparity between national laws.

Advocate-General Mancini delivered a remarkably vigorous opinion, in which he asserted that the rules should be regarded as justified despite their restrictive effect on trade in pasta products.

---

27. Case 27/80 *Fietje* [1980] ECR 3839. See also Commission Communication concerning the use of languages in the marketing of foodstuffs in the light of the judgment in Case C-369/89 *Piageme v Peeters* [1991] ECR I-2971. More generally, on a 'positive' Community approach to labelling, Council Resolution on future action on the labelling of products in the interest of the consumer, OJ 1993 C110/1.
28. Case 407/85 [1988] ECR 4233.

He explained that Italians like their pasta *al dente*, 'glissant des deux côtés de la fourchette'.[29] These properties derive from manufacture using durum wheat alone, as envisaged under the challenged Italian law. But should this be enough to justify the Italian authorities denying consumers a choice of rather more prosaic pasta? The Advocate-General referred to the principle that it is impermissible to ban a particular type of product where the consumer can be adequately informed about its composition by labelling rules. He inspected four packets of pasta – Italian, Belgian, German and Swiss – acquired in a Luxembourg supermarket. All bore the word 'spaghetti'; all had a range of further information about their varying composition, some 'in microscopic letters'. Mr Mancini concluded that an Italian consumer could *not* be adequately informed by labels about production of differently constituted pasta in other states, given the depth of cultural expectation in Italy about pasta, its many forms of presentation and the exclusive use of durum wheat. Mr Mancini was keenly aware of the institutional choices at stake. His view was that the matter should be resolved through the introduction of common rules by legislative act. Market liberalization achieved through negative law would wreck the market structure for durum wheat production, while also causing undue consumer confusion (the other side of the coin from consumer choice).

Mr Mancini's view did not prevail. The Court came to the opposite conclusion. It found the Italian rules unjustified. It did not investigate in any depth the matters that had so troubled its Advocate-General. It observed that it remained open to the Italian authorities to restrict the description 'pasta made from durum wheatmeal' to pasta products made exclusively from durum wheat, and thereby to inform the consumer. The consequence of the ruling is that non-Italian producers could sell their goods in Italy and the Italian consumer could choose from a wider range of pastas. It appears to be assumed by the Court that a consumer will be able satisfactorily to grasp the differences between available pasta products. The Court's ruling applies the Cassis de Dijon principle as a means of achieving market integration without waiting for the slow wheels of the

---

29. Mr Mancini draws this description from the Journal of André Gide, 22 June 1942; ECR 4253.

Community legislative machinery to turn. Whereas the Advocate-General doubted the workability of a market based solely on mutual recognition, and would have upheld state decisions taken on behalf of consumers pending Community legislative intervention, the Court's ruling is based on an implied expectation that an informed consumer is capable of making a proper choice.

Consumer choice in the deregulated wider market *versus* the protection at national level of the economic interests of consumers

National rules designed to protect consumers' economic interests may impede trade where they differ state by state. This may affect several different techniques of national consumer protection, including the suppression of misleading product descriptions, the exclusion of unfair competition and the prohibition of misleading advertising. The impediment arises where the use of a technique employed in state A is forbidden in state B, which forces the trader to pursue a different strategy especially for state B. Where that happens, the importer into state B is forced to adapt and is therefore at a disadvantage compared to state B's own traders. This is sufficient to trigger Article 30.

National rules are based on notions of deception which differ state by state. 'Hard sell' in one state may be 'unfair sell' in another. The Court's jurisprudence provides a window on distinct national views of what should and should not be allowed of traders seeking to drum up business. This then allows an appreciation of the Court's own view of the permitted level of legal protection that may be afforded by the national system in an integrating market. The case law vividly portrays the problematic collision between competing aspects of the consumer interest. The examination that follows contrasts three decisions in which the Court prioritized the consumer interest in integration and wider choice by ruling national measures of (alleged) consumer protection incompatible with Article 30 with three further decisions in which the Court reached the opposite conclusion by upholding national measures of market regulation despite the damage they caused to the elaboration of an integrated commercial strategy for the Community market. In all these cases, directly or indirectly, the Court is forced to engage in an assessment of how the market serves the consumer.

Unlawful national rules governing the protection of the economic interests of consumers

GB-INNO v CCL[30] involved a challenge to a Luxembourg law which controlled the provision by a trader of information about prices of goods. Advertising practices permitted in Belgium were precluded by this stricter Luxembourg law. This disparity between national laws made it difficult for GB-INNO to develop an integrated marketing strategy for the Belgo-Luxembourg market. It fell to Luxembourg to justify the laws. It was unable to convince the European Court. The Court was unpersuaded by the notion that the consumer might benefit from suppression of information. The Court referred to the 1981 Resolution adopting a Consumer Protection and Information Policy in asserting the close connection between consumer protection and consumer information.[31] It is of constitutional interest that the Court drew in this way on a soft law instrument adopted a long time prior to the formalization of Community competence in the field of consumer protection.

Schutzverband gegen Unwesen in der Wirtschaft v Y. Rocher GmbH[32] displays a similar policy preference in favour of a free market in information allied to a free market in goods. German law prohibited advertisements in which individual prices were compared, except where the comparison was not eyecatching. Rocher showed that the rule inhibited its ability to construct an integrated marketing strategy because it could not export to Germany techniques used elsewhere in states with more liberal laws. The European Court focused on the fact that the German law controlled eyecatching advertisements whether or not they were true. The law suppressed the supply of accurate information to the consumer. The Court's ruling leaves no room for doubt that such a restriction cannot find justification under Community law.

The interplay between judicial decisions and legislation in the Community is well illustrated here. Directive 84/450 harmonizes national laws concerning misleading advertising. That, however,

---

30. Case C-362/88 [1990] ECR I-667.   31. See Chapter 1, p.11.
32. Case C-126/91 judgment of 18 May 1993.

was all that remained of a more ambitious original proposal to regulate misleading and unfair advertising and to liberalize comparative advertising.[33] The unfair and comparative elements had to be deleted in the face of inability to achieve agreement on a Community regime in the face of severe heterogeneity among national laws. German law was strict in its control, English law, for example, much less so. Yet comparative advertising has now been opened up by the Court's 'negative law' rulings in *GB-INNO* and *Rocher*. This shows how national systems may be forced to adjust under the influence of EC law even where legislative initiatives are blocked.

The third case in this series is *Verband Sozialer Wettbewerb eV v Clinique Laboratories SNC*.[34] German law prohibited the use of the name 'Clinique' for cosmetics, because of an alleged risk that consumers would be misled into believing the products had medicinal properties. Klinik is the German word for hospital. This ban was held to impede trade in goods marketed in other member states under the Clinique name. It fell to Germany to show justification for the rule, but it was unable to do this to the Court's satisfaction. The Court was not persuaded that there was sufficient likelihood of consumer confusion for a barrier to trade to be justified. Cosmetics were not sold in outlets specializing in pharmaceutical products. Consumers in other states, with less restrictive regimes, did not seem to encounter confusion. The Court here invites the retort that consumers in other states do not face the risk of confusing Clinique and Klinik, for this is peculiar to the German language. This point could be developed into a more general criticism that the Court is making sweeping assumptions about the capacity of the 'European consumer' to operate confidently in the market which are divorced from special circumstances that may prevail in particular parts of the Community. German law, in particular, has been exposed as 'over-regulatory' in the view of the Court,[35] but there have been disgruntled responses from some German lawyers accusing the

---

[33.] OJ 1978 C70/4, amended proposal OJ 1979 C194/3. See N. Reich, 'Protection of Consumers' Economic Interests by the EC' 14 Sydney Law Rev 23 (1992), p. 33.

[34.] Case C-315/92 [1994] ECR I-317.

[35.] See also Case C-470/93 *Verein gegen Unwesen in Handel und Gewerbe Köln eV v Mars GmbH* [1995] ECR I-1923. Cf. under Art. 59 Case 76/90 *M. Säger v Dennemeyer and Co. Ltd* [1991] ECR I-4221.

Court of failure to take adequate account of national experience in identifying commercial practices which may prejudice at least *some* consumers.[36] The European Court seems to envisage a rather robust, self-reliant consumer in the market who is able to enjoy the fruits of integration. Such a perspective requires the relaxation of the grip of national laws based on a conception of a consumer more gullible than the European Court will acknowledge.

Yet other cases suggest a greater readiness on the part of the Court to accept that a free flow of marketing practices may not be achieved by virtue of the application of Article 30. These cases suggest less faith in the competence of the individual consumer in the market.

Lawful national rules governing the protection of the economic interests of consumers

Oosthoek's Uitgeversmaatschappij[37] involved rules imposed in the Netherlands which controlled the offer of free gifts as an inducement to purchase encyclopaedias. Sellers from outside the Netherlands who were accustomed to using such marketing methods were forced to alter their strategy for the Dutch market. Integration was impeded.[38] The Court conceded that the banned marketing techniques may result in consumers being misled. It ruled that it was, accordingly, possible to justify the Dutch rules as measures necessary to prevent deception and to enhance consumer protection and fair trading, encompassing the protection of the honest trader from unfair competition. National rules which prevent producers pursuing unfair commercial practices may be compatible with Article 30 even where they forbid the deployment of tactics that are permitted elsewhere in the Community. The ruling confirms that Community law does not drive down standards of protection to the lowest common denominator among the member states.

---

36. H. Piper, 'Zu den Answirkungen des EG-Binnenmarktes auf das deutsche Recht gegen den unlauteren Wettbewerb' Wettbewerb in Recht und Praxis 685 (1992): cf. discussion by O. Sosnitza in *Wettbewerbsbeschränkungen durch die Rechtsprechung* (Baden-Baden, Nomos, 1995), ch. 4.
37. Case 286/81 [1982] ECR 4575.
38. This is probably enough to cross even the *Keck and Mithouard* threshold for the invocation of Art. 30, especially in the light of the *Clinique* ruling.

The same acceptance on the part of the Court that the consumer may be unable properly to process information and that, accordingly, member states may be able to offer protection even where that impedes the process of market integration emerges from the ruling in *Buet v Ministère Public*[39] in which the Court held that a French law which prohibited 'doorstep selling' of educational material was not incompatible with Article 30 in view of its contribution to the protection of consumer from pressure selling tactics. Nor was the legislation preempted by the 'Doorstep Selling' Directive, for that Directive is 'minimum' in character.[40]

It is obviously the case that laws which suppress deliberately misleading practices will survive scrutiny in the light of Article 30. Indeed, the Community has itself entered the field of legal control of misleading advertising.[41] However, the laws at issue in *Oosthoek* and in *Buet* controlled techniques which need not be deceptive to an alert consumer, but which might have misled a consumer unfamiliar with the technique. The cases display a more permissibly paternalist approach to the consumer than that which emerges from *GB-INNO*, *Rocher* and *Clinique*.

In *Alpine Investments v Minister van Financiën*[42] a rather different situation arose. The ruling is significant on many levels, including the important reminder that market regulation may pursue the objective of consumer protection at the same time as establishing standards of proper conduct in order to forestall rogue traders undermining the reputation of the majority of participants in the market. The case concerned Dutch rules placing a restriction on the practice of 'cold calling' potential consumers of financial services. The rule applied to all providers of services established in the Netherlands and restricted the opportunity to drum up business from customers both in the Netherlands and beyond its borders. The Court declared that 'such a prohibition deprives the operators concerned of a rapid and direct technique for marketing and for contacting potential clients in other member states. It can therefore constitute a restriction on the freedom to provide cross-border services'. Given this impediment to direct access to the market of another member state, the rule required justification. One might have supposed

---

[39.] Case 328/87 [1989] ECR 1235.   [40.] Chapter 3.   [41.] Chapter 6.
[42.] Case C-384/93 [1995] ECR I-1141.

that protection of the consumer from unsolicited telephone calls would form the basis of a justification, which would have required consideration of the extent to which consumers can be expected to look after themselves when confronted by such marketing. However, the Court refused to adopt this approach. It would not accept that the Netherlands could claim jurisdiction to protect consumers in other states, even though it was forced to concede that a home state regulator is much better placed to achieve supervision than a target state regulator. But, viewing the Dutch rules from a different perspective in order to avoid treating them as extraterritorial in effect, it found that the protection of the reputation of Dutch firms in the sector could count as a justification for the rules. The Court did not accept that the fact that authorities in other member states were more liberal in their approach to supervision of such marketing techniques rendered the Dutch ban disproportionate. From this perspective, the ruling rejects negative law as a method for fixing the permissible regulation of the Community market at the lowest common denominator of national protection. In effect, the Court was prepared to permit the Dutch authorities to put their own traders at a disadvantage by denying them the capacity to use 'cold calling' as a method of building a cross-border commercial strategy. However, it is plain that the establishment of a Community-wide system of consumer protection could be achieved only by positive law, through Community legislative action. Moreover, effective enforcement of regulation of such activity would require close co-operation between authorities in different states in view of the technology involved, which transcends physical borders.

Towards a European consumer?

One must appreciate the context in which the Court makes these assessments in order to avoid overstating the potential for drawing a common European notion of the consumer from these cases. The Court is assessing the validity of national choices, not directly imposing its own standard. So, for example, *Buet* represents an acceptance that the French authorities may protect their consumers where other states see no such need. The Court is not saying in *Buet* that the French consumer is particularly gullible, but rather that the French authorities are entitled to take that view in conformity with Community law. Perceptions of the consumer vary between the different legal systems of the member states and this remains permissible within the limits which the Court has evolved for checking national regulatory choices. That limit is reached where the Court identifies 'over-regulation' of the market; where, as in *GB-INNO*, *Rocher* and *Clinique*, the Court believes consumer choice in the wider market should prevail over perceived risk of prejudice to economic interests. In such circumstances, the Court's expectation of basic consumer competence in the market prompts it to find such national rules incompatible with Community law. Accordingly, the presence of a large block of prudent consumers who will not be duped by a particular practice undermines the legitimacy of national measures designed to suppress that practice, even where some gullible consumers would be prejudiced. This is critically important to the thesis of this book: that a Community notion of the 'consumer' is beginning to emerge, albeit indirectly in this instance, in the context of checking the validity of national measures which restrict trade.

In some cases where the Court has upheld national rules of consumer protection in spite of its more typical assumption of a 'reasonably circumspect' consumer,[43] the Court has mentioned that a special type of consumer is the subject of protection. So it was of significance that in *Buet* the national law was designed to protect consumers behind with their education and wishing to improve it. By contrast, in *Rocher*, for example, there were no such special considerations; the national rule simply prevented consumers finding out (accurate) information. Further illumination of the Court's stance may be gleaned from *Säger v Dennemeyer*,[44] in which the Court refused to accept that German rules, which had the effect of restricting choice of out-of-state providers of services connected with patent renewal, could be justified, pointing out that in any event a flawed service would not severely prejudice the buyer. Even a failure to renew a patent by the deadline did not exclude the possibility of subsequent renewal, albeit subject to payment of a small penalty fee. By analogy, one would presume that the graver the risk of harm to the consumer, the stronger the case for regulation of a particular

---

43. Para. 24 of the ruling in *Mars*, note 35, above.
44. Case C-76/90 [1991] ECR 4221.

commercial practice or activity. Indeed, in cases concerning insurance provision, the Court has been noticeably more receptive to the permissibility of national regulations, even where they impede the activities of out-of-state companies.[45] Removal of trade barriers caused by divergence between justified national systems of supervision is a matter for the legislature, and common Community-wide rules governing the standards required of providers of financial services have been agreed in a number of sectors in recent years.[46]

Mutual recognition has replaced positive harmonization established through Community rules in many circumstances as a consequence of the Court's vigorous renovation of Article 30, beginning with the Cassis de Dijon ruling. National methods of consumer protection must be adjusted in the light of the impermissibility of maintaining the isolation of national markets. However, in pursuit of market integration, there remains a need for Community legislative initiatives in the field of consumer protection where national rules remain justified. Broader still, there may be arguments in favour of consumer protection laws that are disconnected from the imperatives of market integration. Much of the rest of this book examines legislative developments. However, the nature and purpose of positive Community consumer policy will be seen to be affected by the background impact of negative law on national competence to maintain consumer protection laws.

[45] E.g. Case 205/84 *Commission v Germany* [1986] ECR 3755.
[46] Chapter 3.

CHAPTER THREE

Market transparency and consumer protection

Choice of regulatory technique

Requiring that the consumer be provided with specified information about a contemplated transaction is a regulatory technique that has enjoyed some popularity in the development of EC measures affecting protection of consumers' economic interests.[1] This approach to improving transparency in the pre-contractual phase has frequently been combined with protection in the post-contractual phase, most strikingly through the prescription of a 'cooling-off' period, within which the consumer is entitled to exercise a right to withdraw from an agreed deal.

These techniques do not address directly the content of the bargain between trader and consumer. Contractual terms remain to be fixed by private negotiation. The assumption underlying the type of regulatory technique examined in this chapter is that an imbalance in economic power can be sufficiently corrected by adjusting the environment within which the bargain is struck by giving the consumer extra information in advance and extra time to consider the implications.

There is much to be said for these techniques as forms of regulation which minimize interference with private autonomy. Viewed in their most favourable light, they yield a more efficient market by promoting negotiation and informed consumer choice, without substituting public decision making about the contents of contracts for private choice. More intrusive controls, such as a

---

[1.] S. Weatherill, 'The role of the informed consumer in EC Law and Policy' 2 Consumer Law J 49 (1994). Information disclosure is occasionally employed as a technique to address health and safety issues too; e.g. Directive 89/622 on the labelling of tobacco products, Chapter 6.

ban on particular types of contract, may unduly diminish consumer choice. To assert a power directly to check the validity of particular terms may distort the market, for example by dissuading traders from offering a wide choice.

Nevertheless, these techniques may be criticized for a failure to address substantive unfairness. Tinkering with the process of negotiation will be regarded as of peripheral importance if one holds the view that the consumer, however well supported by mandatory information disclosure, is unable to wrest a fair deal from the economically powerful supplier. Indeed, if a bargaining environment is fundamentally flawed by the imbalance between the parties, then to introduce disclosure requirements may even legitimize a pernicious practice. Better, from this standpoint, not to regulate at all than to regulate at the margins and to pretend a solution has been found. Moreover, in the specific context of EC harmonization, there is a suspicion that harmonization at the level of information provision, rather than direct control of contract content, represents the line of least political resistance. An inability to agree contentious proposals to set basic minimum standards of fairness applicable to contract terms may cause agreement to be deflected to less controversial aspects of information disclosure. Aspects of EC consumer policy are, like many areas of any legislature's output, the result of political expediency rather than considered selection among available regulatory techniques.

These introductory observations are pitched at a rather broad level. Naturally, assessment of Community practice depends on awareness of the particular nature of consumer problems which arise in a range of sectors. In addition, underlying questions of political perception of the place of freedom and fairness in a market economy dictate one's attitude to the appropriate intensity of regulation of the contract.[2] The remainder of this chapter examines the pattern of existing Community legislation in the field.

Consumer credit

There are two Community measures affecting the legal regulation of the supply of consumer credit. Directive 87/102 was the

---

[2.] T. Wilhelmsson, *Social Contract Law and European Integration* (Aldershot, Dartmouth, 1994).

Community's first venture into the field and this was followed by amending Directive 90/88.[3] Both Directives harmonize national measures in the field and are based on the perception that differences between member state laws governing the supply of consumer credit distort competition between grantors of credit and impede consumers from obtaining credit in other member states. Harmonization is required in order to integrate the market for goods and services obtainable by consumers on credit. Accordingly, Directive 87/102 is based on Article 100 EC, while amending Directive 90/88, a post-Single European Act initiative, takes Article 100a EC as its legal base.

A central issue in any system of consumer credit regulation is the definition of the types of transaction which are subject to the rules in question. Article 1(1) provides simply that the Directive 'applies to credit agreements'. This is elaborated in Article 1(2), which offers amplification of the terms 'consumer'; 'creditor'; 'credit agreement'; 'total cost of the credit to the consumer'; and 'annual percentage rate of charge'. Article 2 provides exclusions for a variety of transactions. Article 2(1) covers deals to which the Directive is not applicable; Articles 2(2) and (4) permit member states to opt to exempt further types of deal.

Leaving aside such matters of detail, the key to understanding the approach favoured by these measures lies in their evident concern to improve transparency, so that the consumer is more fully aware of the costs of credit which he or she contemplates purchasing. The Recitals to the Directive assert that 'the consumer should receive adequate information on the conditions and cost of credit and on his obligations'. Article 3 of Directive 87/102 is central to the policy of information disclosure. It is aimed at ensuring that an advertisement or offer displayed at business premises involving an offer of credit and in which figures relating to costs are indicated shall include 'a statement of the annual percentage rate of charge'. Article 4(1) provides that 'Credit agreements shall be made in writing. The consumer shall receive a copy of the written agreement'. That written agreement shall include matters listed in Article 4(2), which includes a statement of the annual percentage rate of charge. Article 1(4) of amending Directive 90/88 adds two further subparagraphs to Article 4(2). Article 4(3) of Directive 87/102 provides that 'The

3. OJ 1987 L42/48, OJ 1990 L61/14, respectively.

written agreement shall further include the other essential terms of the contract'. This notion is not exhaustively defined. It is elaborated by an illustrative list of essential terms in an Annex to the Directive, which became Annex I as a result of amending Directive 90/88. The scope of the requirement under Articles 3 and 4 to declare the annual percentage rate of charge is limited by Article 5. Member states which, at the time of notification of the Directive, do not require the annual percentage rate of charge to be shown or which do not have an established method for its calculation, 'shall at least require the total cost of the credit to the consumer to be indicated'. However, Article 5 declares that this is to apply 'pending a decision on the introduction of a Community method or methods of calculating the annual percentage rate of charge' and this matter was addressed in amending Directive 90/88. That Directive asserts the desirability of providing 'that one method of calculating the said annual percentage rate of charge should be used throughout the Community' and is directed to the creation of an appropriate mathematical formula which can be used for this purpose. The appropriate amendments to Directive 87/102 were made by Directive 90/88, including the insertion of a new Article 1a and two further Annexes, Annexes II and III, which are directed to this end. Certain transitional periods were incorporated, stated to expire at the latest at the end of 1995, when a Council decision adopted on the basis of a Commission proposal was to cause the introduction of a single Community mathematical formula for calculating the annual percentage rate of charge. This was delayed, according to the Commission, as a result of the 1995 enlargement of the Union and the slow transposition of Directives 87/102 and 90/88 by some member states, and the interim pattern will remain in place pending agreement in Council and Parliament in accordance with Article 189b EC.[4]

Article 15 of Directive 87/102 incorporates the 'minimum harmonization' formula. It states that 'This Directive shall not preclude member states from retaining or adopting more stringent provisions to protect consumers consistent with their obligations under the Treaty'. Existing techniques for protecting consumers, which may be more rigorous than those envisaged by these initiatives, need not be repealed. Nor are states impeded from

4. COM (96) 79.

innovating through new, more stringent regulatory techniques, provided that such intervention is compatible with primary Community law, in particular the Treaty provisions on free movement. The Commission has published information revealing that most member states have gone far beyond the minimum protective standards required by the Directives.[5]

These measures leave largely unaffected the actual cost of credit. The substance of the bargain is in the main untouched, but the environment within which the bargain is made is adjusted by mandatory disclosure of particular types of information. The Directives' constitutional roots in the policy of market integration via Articles 100 and 100a identify them as contributions to the process of integrating the market for financial services, but the terms on which such integration is to be achieved include mandatory transparency. So, subject to the existence of stricter national laws, credit may still be acquired by consumers on terms involving alarmingly high interest repayments, a notorious problem in this area. But, in theory, where high prices are payable under a contract, that will have occurred as a result of free and informed consumer choice between competing suppliers. The technique of information disclosure will, on a favourable interpretation, have improved the operation of the market without going so far as to rob the market of competition and consumer choice by, for example, fixing prices or limiting sources of supply by imposing a prior licensing system.

The Commission's 1995 report on the operation of the regime floats ideas for deeper intervention.[6] Although the Commission argues that a consumer aware of prices can spur the market to more efficient operation, it concedes that over-indebtedness, a problem which has stimulated responses at national level, may require action at Community level. It also observes that consumers enjoy no 'cooling-off' period, in contrast to other EC measures dealing with economic interests discussed in this chapter. The report prompted a rather anodyne Council Resolution,[7] but the consumer aspect of financial services is one of ten priorities set out in the 1996–98 action plan,[8] so the Commission may not be deterred from making formal proposals for reform.

---

5. COM (95) 117, report on the operation of Directive 87/102.
6. Note 5, above.   7. 9 November 1995, not yet published.   8. Chapter 1.

Cross-border financial transactions – soft law to hard law

The structure of the banking market in the Community has been dictated by the existence of different currencies in the member states. The industry has largely been split along national lines. However, the level of cross-border financial activity has inevitably increased in accordance with the integration of the market for goods and services. The complexity of such transactions, involving intermediary institutions and currency exchange, may cause extra cost and time in comparison with purely national deals. In 1990 the Commission issued a Recommendation on the transparency of banking conditions relating to cross-border financial transactions.[9] It is a further example of the importance attributed by the Commission to consumer information.

It is recommended that member states 'ensure that institutions which undertake cross-border financial transactions within the meaning of the Recommendation apply the principles set out in the Annex'. The Annex declares that 'The aim of the principles set out in this Recommendation is to make more transparent the information supplied . . .' Six principles are listed. The majority are directed at aspects of provision of information to the consumer of banking services.

Several member states impose binding rules in the area of transparency of banking conditions. The Preamble to the Recommendation states that '[i]t does not appear expedient to ask those member states to amend their legislation by inserting rules relating solely to cross-border transactions'. It adds that a number of member states wish to retain proven cooperation procedures in the field. Accordingly, the soft law approach, encouraging voluntary cooperation, is preferred. This lighter regulatory touch conforms to interpretations of the subsidiarity principle.[10]

Further investigation followed, revealing, inter alia, that the average cost of a cross-border financial transfer was approximately eighteen per cent of the sum transferred. The Commission remained unhappy with the intransparent state of the market and continued to seek to achieve improvement

[9] Rec. 90/109, OJ 1990 L67/39. [10] Chapter 1, p. 30.

through persuasion. In November 1992 Karel Van Miert, then Consumer Affairs Commissioner, declared that charges still seemed too high and warned that legislation may be required. However, Sir Leon Brittan, the Competition Commissioner until the end of 1992, expressed the view that cooperation would be preferable to legislation. This may serve as an example of the problems in establishing a coherent consumer policy in a Commission which has many different interests to take into account.

After Christiane Scrivener assumed responsibility for Consumer Policy in 1993, monitoring continued. Further study revealed that costs of transferring small sums between states remained high. The Commission maintained an insistence on the importance of transparency and consumer information, but its preference for soft law over proposing the adoption of formal legislation diminished. After a survey carried out in 1994, it concluded that self-regulation by the industry had yielded disappointing results. For example, it was found that written information to customers was completely lacking in nearly half of 352 branches surveyed Union-wide. Of a sample of over 1,000 transfers, double charging occurred in 36 per cent of cases. The average total cost of making a transfer of an amount equivalent to 100 ECU was 25.4 ECU.

The Commission therefore published a draft Directive,[11] which subsequently reappeared as the draft Directive on cross-border credit transfers,[12] based on Article 100a. This proposed initiative addresses issues connected with transparency, suppression of double-charging and delay, and proposes the establishment of minimum performance levels. There are several requirements of transparency, such as the provision of information about the basis for the calculation of commission and charges by the bank. Double-charging would be precluded. In the absence of specific agreement it would be expected that the transfer would be completed in a total of six working days in all (five days at the originator's bank, one day at the beneficiary's bank). The proposal has not yet been formally adopted.

It is instructive to appreciate that the Commission's decision to shift away from issuing soft law instruments to proposing formal legislation conforms fully to the principle of subsidiarity. Although one might properly interpret subsidiarity as meaning that soft law should be preferred over hard law where both are

---

11. OJ 1994 C360/13.   12. OJ 1995 C199/16.

equally effective in achieving the end in view, once the inadequacies of soft law have been demonstrated, pursuit of the stipulated objective through binding legal instruments becomes appropriate.

'Doorstep selling'

Directive 85/577 is concerned with the harmonization of laws concerning the protection of the consumer in respect of contracts negotiated away from business premises.[13] It is more commonly known as the 'Doorstep Selling Directive'. It is based on Article 100 EC, although its explanation of the need to achieve harmonization in the field in pursuit of the integration of the market is extraordinarily terse. Contracts between a trader and a consumer are commonly concluded away from the trader's business premises. Legislation governing such deals differs from state to state. In fact, states vary in their choice of public or private law to control such activities. The Recitals to the Directive declare that disparities may directly affect the functioning of the common market and accordingly claim a rationale for approximation of laws in the field. More than most measures, this Directive demonstrates that, under Treaty provisions such as Article 100, which require unanimous agreement in Council, political agreement is the key and explanation of economic rationales for action have tended to become little more than constitutional formality in the Community.

In line with the measures affecting the supply of credit, examined above, the Doorstep Selling Directive is concerned with harmonization of the rules governing the circumstances in which deals are made, and not with the substance of the terms themselves. The Directive does not forbid sales away from business premises, nor does it directly address the content of concluded contracts. It requires that the consumer be allowed a cooling-off period. The consumer has a minimum seven-day period in which to withdraw from a contract concluded in the circumstances defined by the Directive. A fuller definition of the types of contract in issue is provided under Article 1, subject to a list of exceptions in Article 3(2), and the notions of trader and consumer are defined in Article 2.

13. OJ 1985 L372/31.

The control exercised over the defined transactions is contained in Article 4. Traders must give consumers written notice of their right of cancellation in accordance with the procedures in Article 4. Article 5 provides that the right to cancel may be exercised within a set period after the receipt of the Article 4 notice. The period must be not less than seven days from receipt of the notice. According to Article 7, the potentially complex issues of dealing with money or goods which may already have changed hands fall to be dealt with under national law. This is a readily comprehensible acknowledgement of the limits of the 'Europeanization' of private law.

The measure falls firmly within the category of those concerned to improve the consumer's information and bargaining position. The transaction may be concluded on the doorstep and enforced on whatever terms the parties may agree, but the consumer is to be supported in the pre- and post-bargaining phase by information provision and a right to withdraw. This secures consumer choice, but takes account of what the Recitals describe as the 'surprise element' that may taint negotiation away from business premises. So, if a consumer enters into a deal covered by the Directive with a trader who has set up a stall in, say, a railway station, then the Directive, implemented into national law, allows the consumer to re-think the deal and to withdraw within the defined period, which must not be shorter than seven days. The consumer will be able to defeat a breach of contract action brought before national courts by the supplier.[14] The Directive's perception of the need to protect the consumer leads to adjustment of national law of contract formation and, in an admittedly rather peripheral area, brings about a harmonization of private law.

Article 8 of Directive 85/577 stipulates that it is a measure of minimum harmonization. Therefore, the Directive itself does not conclude debate on the regulatory choice that lies between, on the one hand, consumer protection achieved through information provision and, on the other hand, deeper intervention involving outright prohibition of particular practices. The Directive simply

---

14. The choice of the example of a railway station is deliberate: Italy's failure to implement this Directive, combined with the Court's refusal to acknowledge the horizontal direct effect of Directives, lay behind Ms Dori's inability simply to defeat a breach of contract action in the litigation that generated the ruling in Case C-91/92 *Faccini Paola Dori v Recreb Srl*, examined in Chapter 8.

establishes a minimum level of protective regulation, which may be exceeded by states prefering to operate more stringent systems of protection entailing a consequential reduction in consumer choice. It remains necessary for stricter measures which are not pre-empted by the Directive to conform to primary Community law. This interplay between secondary and primary Community law is well illustrated by the Court's ruling in *Buet v Ministère Public*,[15] which additionally serves to illuminate the type of consumer who is recognized as entitled to protection under national or Community law. The case arose as a result of French rules forbidding doorstep selling of particular types of educational material. This plainly exceeded the restrictions on commercial activity imposed by Directive 85/577. However, the Directive's characterization as a measure of minimum harmonization led to the conclusion that the French rules were not pre-empted by Community intervention in the field. The Court then proceeded to rule that even though the ban exerted a restrictive effect on cross-border trade, it was compatible with Article 30 as a contribution to consumer protection justified under Community law. So, even though the Community legislature had not felt the need to introduce a prohibition in the field, it remained open to national authorities to maintain more extensive patterns of intervention in conformity with primary and secondary Community law.

Package travel

Directive 90/314 deals with package travel, package holidays and package tours.[16] It is based on Article 100a. Member states have employed a range of techniques to regulate the package travel industry, including a civil law approach in Germany, administrative regulation in France and an essentially self-regulatory structure in the UK. This pattern of variation has served to prevent the integration of the market. The Directive's objective is the establishment of safeguards for those on package travel, package holidays and package tours. Its primary thrust is directed towards information disclosure, although to a limited

---

15. Case 328/87 [1989] ECR 1235.   16. OJ 1990 L158/59.

extent it affects substance. It adopts the familiar model of minimum harmonization.

Not all travel is included. The Directive concerns only the 'package'. Article 1 defines the 'package' as a holiday lasting more than 24 hours or incorporating overnight accommodation and which includes a combination of at least two other components when sold or offered for sale at an inclusive price. The components are transport; accommodation; or other tourist services, as defined. A simple house rental would not be covered. The consumer entitled to benefit from the Directive includes any person taking or agreeing to take a package, even as part of a business trip.

The measure employs the technique of information disclosure to safeguard consumers of package holidays. Article 3(1) prohibits misleading information. Articles 3(2) and 4(1) address the process of supplying information. Article 3(2) provides that '[w]here a brochure is made available to the consumer, it shall indicate in a legible, comprehensible and accurate manner both the price and adequate information concerning' a list of matters including destination, transport, type of accommodation and itinerary. Article 4(1) provides that the organiser and/or retailer shall provide the consumer, before the conclusion of the contract with general information on passport and visa requirements and required health formalities and, in good time before the start of the journey, with information about, inter alia, details of the organiser and/or retailer's local representative or local agencies or, in any case, 'an emergency telephone number or any other information that will enable him to contract [sic] the organiser and/or the retailer'. Article 4(2) provides that member states shall ensure that, inter alia, 'all the terms of the contract are set out in writing or such other form as is comprehensible and accessible to the consumer and must be communicated to him before the conclusion of the contract'. Moreover, states shall ensure that the consumer is given a copy of these terms.

The Directive makes only a limited incursion into the substance of the bargain. It makes provision for transfer of bookings under Article 4(3), control of price variation under Article 4(4), and compensation for cancellation under Article 4(6). Article 5 provides that the package organizer may be liable not only for its own performance but also for that of the retailer and the supplier. There is a presumption of fault against the operator, but liability is not strict.

Timeshare

The phenomenon of 'timeshare' refers, loosely, to an agreement which allows a consumer use of property for a specified period in the year. The property is, in effect, rented out to a series of consumers, but the arrangement envisages a more long-term relationship than a simple one-off holiday let. Marketing of timeshare has attracted criticism as a result of the perceived use of high-pressure tactics, and national controls have begun to develop. This yields the legislative diversity between states that has commonly been used as a rationale for the introduction of harmonization measures at EC level. It might be added that the sale of timeshare has typically, though not exclusively, involved consumers in one state acquiring an interest in property in another state, which is liable to give rise to serious difficulties in enforcement and complex questions of private international law. Harmonization of laws, especially at a minimum level, cannot fully resolve these problems, but the cross-border features of the timeshare sector make it a particularly appropriate candidate for regulation at transnational level.

The EC entered the field with the adoption of Directive 94/47 on 'protection of purchasers in respect of certain aspects of contracts relating to the purchase of the right to use immovable properties on a timeshare basis'.[17] The legal base is Article 100a EC and, since it is a post-Maastricht measure, it was made jointly by the Council and the Parliament in accordance with the legislative procedure set out in Article 189b.

The pattern of the harmonized system is largely comparable to that employed in relation to doorstep selling. The primary focus of the proposal is improvement in the transparency of the transaction, so that the consumer is aware of the nature of the deal that is being offered. Specified items must be included in the contract, which shall be in writing. The Directive also establishes the right of a consumer to withdraw from a contract for a period after its conclusion, at least ten calendar days in this instance. Member states remain free to impose extra requirements in accordance with the minimum harmonization formula.

More than most measures, the effective application of this Directive as an instrument of consumer protection against

[17.] OJ 1994 L280/83.

unscrupulous commercial tactics depends on ready access to justice. Problems will frequently arise in a cross-border context. The creation of a minimum level of consumer protection will of itself avail the consumer little, if the obstacles to vindication of legal rights are forbiddingly high. Moreover, in so far as such laws are designed to encourage the active consumer to treat the market as extending beyond his or her home state, such inhibition will harm the process of integration. These issues are considered further in Chapter 8.

Distance selling

The notion of 'distance selling' embraces situations where the trader and the consumer are physically separated. Sale by fax, telephone or increasingly available electronic media such as the Internet provide examples. Such techniques reflect technological innovation and they are particularly suited to cross-border trade. Where the subject of the transaction is itself intangible, the crossing of a national frontier becomes quite irrelevant and certainly no effective basis for regulating the conduct of the deal. To this extent, distance selling in the EC is not only a practical inevitability, it is a desirable, pro-integrative development. Nevertheless, such trends may undermine the effective application of laws of market regulation. In response to the need for a common, cross-border pattern of control, reflecting the common, cross-border marketing strategies that are in many sectors firmly in place, the Community has endeavoured to secure agreement on rules regulating 'distance selling'.

The Commission first issued a proposal in 1992, taking Article 100a EC as the legal base.[18] This document is accompanied by an impressively full and helpful background explanation. The perceived risk that prompts intervention in the market is that consumers may not be fully aware of the nature of the transaction. The Commission's proposal for harmonized rules compares with that chosen for control over other selling methods, including doorstep selling. The objective is to achieve

---

18. COM (92) 11, OJ 1992 C156/14.

transparency through mandatory information disclosure and to provide some additional substantive protection. However, there was dispute about the level of intervention envisaged.

In April 1992 the Commission adopted a Recommendation on codes of practice for the protection of consumers in respect of distance selling.[19] It envisages that a Directive will be supplemented by codes of practice applicable to particular forms of communication. It is recommended that trade associations should adopt codes which include a list of points found in an Annex to the Recommendation and that they should secure compliance with the codes by members.

It seems probable that any Directive adopted in the field will be less wide-ranging than originally proposed by the Commission. The Council agreed a common position in 1995[20] on a minimum measure, which envisages mandatory provision of information in advance to consumers regarding, inter alia, the identity of the supplier, the main characteristics of the goods or services and their price. A cooling-off period of no less than seven days is envisaged, which would conform directly to the structure of Directive 85/577. It is proposed that where unsolicited goods are sent to a consumer, a failure to respond shall not constitute consent to the transaction. The majority of member states make similar provision, which is designed to deprive traders of an inducement to secure sales by exploiting consumer inertia. Concerns in Council about the proper scope of the measure are well illustrated by the exclusion from the common position of contracts relating to financial services, even though one might suppose that such transactions are peculiarly well-suited to the use of technological methods in which consumer and supplier are physically distant. The impression of effective lobbying of the political institutions by this sector is confirmed by appreciation that insurance contracts and contracts for securities are already excluded from the scope of the Doorstep Selling Directive. The measure, which requires the support of both Council and Parliament, in accordance with Article 189b, has not yet been finally agreed.

19. OJ 1992 L156/21.   20. OJ 1995 C288/1.

Financial services

The wide sweep of the integration of the market for financial services is treated as lying beyond the scope of this book.[21] In so far as the several Directives which have secured the liberalization of the market for banking, insurance services and investment services in the securities field breed intensified competition and the realization of economies of scale, then they serve the consumer interest in accordance with the standard assumptions of common market theory. However, as examined above, in the particular context of consumer credit, the integration of the market demands that the consumer interest that was previously expressed through national rules must be translated into common rules operating Community-wide. So, for example, the process of establishing an integrated market for banks and insurance companies is based on a system of 'home state control', which means that provided a company is authorized within its home state, it is entitled in principle to do business throughout the Community, within the field covered by that authorization, without finding itself subject to extra regulatory requirements imposed by other states. However, the rules applied by the 'home state' are drawn from Community legislation and include provisions that are designed to guarantee the protection of, inter alia, the consumer, by ensuring supervision of the commercial viability of firms. For example, Community Directives establish requirements relating to capital adequacy, prudential supervision and deposit guarantee schemes. This is indirect consumer law.

This is the law on paper. One of the areas of Community law which has been little tested in practice is the extent to which states fall prey to the temptation to adopt a lax approach to enforcing the rules in order to provide firms based in their territory with competitive advantages over firms based in the territory of more rigorous enforcers. Where the consumers who are likely to be prejudiced by the turning of a blind eye to the application of the law are largely resident in other states, the temptation may be all the greater. Such tendencies, real or even perceived, damage the confidence of both traders and consumers

---

21. J. Usher, *The Law of Money and Financial Services in the EC* (Oxford, OUP, 1994); M. Cremona, 'Freedom of Movement of Financial Services in A. Caiger and D. Floudas (eds) *1996 Onwards* (Chichester, Wiley Chancery, 1996), ch. 5.

in the integrative process. No lawyer should neglect the gulf between the law on paper and the law in practice, and it is at least a working hypothesis that the Community lacks the institutional mechanisms adequately to police such devious strategies.

Concerns about the capacity of the financial services sector adequately to serve the consumer prompted the Commission to issue a Green Paper in 1996, entitled 'Financial Services: Meeting Consumers' Expectations'.[22] This is designed to prompt debate. Moreover, the Commission's 1996–98 action plan places consumer aspects of financial services among ten priorities.[23] Lurking in the future is the enormously important task of ensuring consumer awareness of the implications of economic and monetary union.

[22.] COM (96) 209. [23.] Chapter 1, p. 29.

CHAPTER FOUR

Regulating the substance of consumer transactions

Choice of regulatory technique

Techniques such as information disclosure and cooling-off periods, examined in the last chapter, can be summarized as attempts to use the law to support the consumer in the pre- and post-contractual phase. They aim to make the consumer more fully aware of the nature of the transaction under contemplation; and to provide an opportunity for withdrawal even after the deal has been agreed. So, to the extent provided by the Directives, the consumer is encouraged to think again before contracting and allowed to change his or her mind even after contracting. But the terms of the bargain themselves are unaffected by these measures. The assumption of the technique of information disclosure is that the consumer, armed with a clearer appreciation of what is on offer, will be able to negotiate a deal closer to his or her real preferences. In consequence, the market system will work more efficiently. Cooling-off periods offer a fall-back protection.

Such legal intervention, designed to improve the conduct of the bargaining process, attracts the criticism that it may simply not go far enough to achieve effective protection of the consumer. The technique of informing the consumer assumes, among other things, that the consumer is capable of grasping the nature of the information which is provided. The more complex the product or service and/or the more complex the nature of the information, the less likely it is that the consumer will be able to respond intelligently to information that is provided. It assumes a competitive market in which traders are induced to offer better terms as a result of the consumer's capacity to perceive what is on offer and to shop around. In some markets, at least, this will not correspond to the true operation of the market. Cooling-off periods may end too early to give the consumer a genuine chance to reassess a purchasing decision, and, in any event, even if a right of withdrawal is invoked, in practice it may not help the consumer to renegotiate a better deal. Worse still, if one perceives an endemic likelihood of exploitation as a result of the differential between the economic power of the trader and that of the consumer, then tinkering with the negotiating process may be regarded as worse than doing nothing, for it will disguise and thus legitimize the fundamental unfairness of the outcome of a system based on contractual freedom, even where spuriously 'informed'. This combination of reasons may lead one to suppose that in some degree the law needs to move beyond adjustment of the bargaining environment towards regulation of the terms of the bargain themselves.

However, the extra step of using the law directly to address the 'fairness' of a contract is controversial on several levels. Most of all, it represents an assault on the notion of freedom of contract – that parties have autonomy to enter into bargains as they see fit, to fix terms as they choose and to expect the law to protect and enforce agreements that have been freely entered into. To use the law to alter bargains struck by private parties may, on some accounts, damage commercial confidence in the reliability of the law, and thus hamper the operation of a market economy. More politically, such intervention attracts criticism for its challenge to individual freedom. However, in the consumer sphere in particular, it has been recognized in recent decades that notions of the purity of contractual freedom are not necessarily consistent with the reality of modern market conditions. In a world of mass-production of technologically advanced products and services, provided through extended distribution chains which leave the consumer remote from the producer and, typically, subject to contractual terms contained in the small print of standard-form contracts, the idea of free negotiation is a myth. The bargain has lost its sanctity as an expression of individual will. Contracts, indeed, may be mass-produced, just as goods are. There remain widely divergent views on the appropriate legal responses to such commercial development, but there is a general acceptance that contractual freedom cannot be viewed in the same light today as it was 50 or more years ago. As a general observation, a willingness to use the law to check some aspects of the *content* of a contract, rather than simply the process of its formation, has evolved.

Directive 93/13 on unfair terms in consumer contracts

These are policy debates that have been played out in many national systems in recent years. Community law, too, has broken through the barrier separating regulation designed to achieve 'mere' procedural fairness from regulation addressing substantive fairness. Directive 93/13 on unfair terms in consumer contracts[1] is applicable to all contracts concluded after 31 December 1994. This remarkable Directive has a scope that is, admittedly, limited in some detailed respects. However, its general impact is highly significant. Sweeping beyond the relatively minor tinkering with the fundamentals of the law of contract formation resulting from the measures covered in the previous chapter, Directive 93/13 is properly regarded as the first incursion of Community law into the heartland of national contract law thinking. This makes it a challenge for national private lawyers, expected to adapt to Community law method after decades of perceiving Community law as, more or less, an enterprise engaged in creating new or extended patterns of public law. But Directive 93/13 is a challenge for Community lawyers too, for, under the camouflage of the harmonization programme, the Directive takes the EC system into largely uncharted private law territory.

The Directive was almost 20 years in the making. The Consumers Consultative Committee expressed a desire for Community action against unfair contract terms in 1977.[2] The Parliament called for a Directive in 1980.[3] Within the Commission, work in the field began in the late 1970s, although it was not until 1984 that its first official document, a discussion paper, was published.[4] Revised proposals based on Article 100a EC emerged thereafter in 1990 and 1992.[5] The proposals, in their several different forms, provoked often heated debate both about

[1]. OJ 1993 L95/29.   [2]. CCC 48/77.   [3]. OJ 1980 C 291/35.
[4]. COM (84) 55, *Unfair Terms in Contracts concluded with Consumers.*
[5]. OJ 1990 C243/2, OJ 1992 C73/7.

the competence of the Community to legislate in the field and the desirability of the details of particular proposals.[6] A number of the member states possess legislation in the field of unfair contract terms, but the control techniques employed are diverse. Some legal systems, including that in the UK, control certain types of clause in certain types of contract directly. The Unfair Contract Terms Act 1977 renders some terms of consumer contracts void, while subjecting others to a test of reasonableness applied by the ordinary courts. In Germany, a law of 1976 sets out a detailed black-list of terms which are void and a 'grey-list' of terms which are capable of being declared void in certain circumstances. In France, by contrast, the matter is dealt with through administrative procedures. A committee makes recommendations to the competent minister, which may lead to legislation against the use of particular terms.

The significant variation in legal technique between the member states makes the case for harmonization under Article 100/100a. But the attempt in practice to find common principles in order to put in place a measure of harmonization at EC level was predictably problematic. That the Directive as finally agreed operates as a minimum measure, allowing states flexibility to apply or maintain more stringent measures of consumer protection, will be no surprise to the observer of the pattern of legal harmonization in this area. Naturally, and, perhaps, gratifyingly, the use of the minimum formula places limits on the extent to which the Directive undermines existing national contract law tradition. However, the compromises required to secure agreement in Council involved more than the mere inclusion of the minimum harmonization clause. It also proved necessary to abandon some aspects of the early proposals in the field before agreement was finally secured in March 1993 and the Directive was adopted. In many respects it is an extraordinarily ambitious measure, albeit less ambitious than some might have hoped. Most of all, it opens up a new potential 'growth area' – European (or at least EC) private law.

[6.] An especially illuminating contribution is that of H. Brandner and P. Ulmer in 'The Community Directive on Unfair Terms in Consumer Contracts' 28 CMLRev 615 (1991), which severely criticizes an earlier draft from a German perspective.

'Unfairness' under Directive 93/13

Proceeding from an assumption of imbalance in the supplier/ consumer relationship, the Directive requires the member states to provide that unfair terms shall not bind the consumer. This is a direct check on the enforceability of contractual terms, and not simply a method of encouraging the consumer to bargain for a better deal and/or to reject an unacceptable deal.

The key to the Directive is its approach to the identification of unfairness. According to Article 3, a term covered by the Directive shall be regarded as unfair if, 'contrary to the requirement of good faith, it causes a significant imbalance in the parties' rights and obligations arising under the contract, to the detriment of the consumer'. An Annex to the Directive provides an indicative and non-exhaustive list of the terms which may be regarded as unfair. This, then, is neither a black- nor a white- but a grey-list. National courts and tribunals may use it as an interpretative aid. This is an aspect of the measure which altered as negotiation progressed. Earlier drafts proposed a black-list, but in the face of disagreement this was abandoned.

It is plain that the elaboration provided by the grey-list in the Annex will be of great significance in the practical application of the system by national courts. The list includes seventeen terms. They are a mixed bag, but not a random collection. There are linking themes.[7] By implication, targets at which the system is aimed seem to include unilateral decision making power claimed by a supplier, a lack of proportionality in the nature of the obligations, and an absence of information provided to the consumer. Where a term imports such deficiencies into the bargain, then it is ripe for characterization as 'unfair' within the meaning of the Directive, which will cause it to be regarded as unenforceable. Terms which illustrate the notion of unilateral decision making include '(f): authorizing the seller or supplier to dissolve the contract on a discretionary basis where the same facility is not granted to the consumer, or permitting the seller or supplier to retain the sums paid for services not yet supplied by him where it is the seller or supplier himself who dissolves the

---

7. T. Wilhelmsson, 'Control of Unfair Contract Terms and Social Values: EC and Nordic Approaches' 16 JCP 435 (1993); C. Willett. 'Directive on Unfair Terms in Consumer Contracts' Consum LJ 114 (1994).

contract'; or '(j): enabling the seller or supplier to alter the terms of the contract unilaterally without a valid reason which is specified in the contract'. Terms suggesting lack of proportionality include '(e): requiring any consumer who fails to fulfil his obligation to pay a disproportionately high sum in compensation'. Threads which provide an incentive to improve transparency and consumer information on pain of holding terms unfair and unenforceable may be traced in '(i): irrevocably binding the consumer to terms with which he had no real opportunity of becoming acquainted before the conclusion of the contract'.

To repeat, the appearance in a contract of a term included in the Annex does not *automatically* mean it is an unfair term; the particular circumstances must always be examined. Article 4 of the Directive provides that unfairness shall be assessed 'taking into account the nature of the goods or services for which the contract was concluded and by referring, at the time of conclusion of the contract, to all the circumstances attending the conclusion of the contract . . .'. It would be to misapprehend the illustrative nature of a grey-list to treat its contents as a group of inevitably indefensible terms. Nevertheless, it is probable that in practice those seeking to defend terms falling within the grey-list before national courts and tribunals will find that they face a difficult task. At the same time, reference to notions such as 'disproportionately' high sums in term (e) and 'undue' restriction in term (q) in the grey-list make plain the discretion vested in judges asked to examine particular terms in their context. More generally, in so far as the Directive is correctly analysed as having as its theoretical base a suspicion about matters such as unilateral decision making power, lack of proportionality and lack of information, it creates an instrument for strengthening the consumer's contractual position by offering protection against the enforcement of unfairly prejudicial terms.

Unfairness and price

The most fundamental unfairness faced by a contracting consumer might be thought to be the risk that he or she will find that the price is too high. But the Directive does *not* permit a consumer to argue that this central term of the contract is unfair.

According to Article 4, 'assessment of the unfair nature of the terms shall relate neither to the definition of the main subject matter of the contract nor to the adequacy of the price and remuneration, on the one hand, as against the services or goods supplies [*sic*] in exchange, on the other, in so far as these terms are in plain intelligible language'. This is a rather obscure formulation. Rather more helpfully, it is explained in the Recitals to the Directive that 'assessment of unfair character shall not be made of terms which describe the main subject matter of the contract nor the quality/price ratio of the goods or services supplied; . . . the main subject matter of the contract and the price/quality ratio may nevertheless be taken into account in assessing the fairness of other terms'. It seems, then, that unfairness does not arise simply where goods or services are overpriced, provided the relevant terms are in plain intelligible language. This limitation to the scope of application of the Directive acts as an important constraint on the power of a judge to assess unfairness in a consumer contract.

Unfairness and good faith

Article 3's linkage of unfairness to the concept of an outcome 'contrary to the requirement of good faith' is likely to prove difficult to handle.[8] Its content will depend on the nature of the bargain. The Preamble to the Directive invites consideration of the strength of the bargaining power of the parties and of whether the consumer was induced to agree to the term. The notion of good faith is familiar in German civil law, but far less accessible to the English private lawyer. This seems likely to impede the development of a common approach to the Article 3 test. Yet unfairness and good faith are prime candidates for 'Europeanization' via the use of the Article 177 preliminary reference procedure.[9] In so far as the European Court is offered and accepts invitations to supply a common interpretation of

---

8. H. Collins, 'Good Faith in European Contract Law' 14 Oxford JLS 229 (1994); M. Tenreiro, 'The Community Directive on Unfair Terms and National Legal Systems' 3 European Review of Private Law 273 (1995).
9. S. Weatherill, 'Prospects for the Development of European Private Law through Europeanisation in the European Court of Justice' 3 European Review of Private Law 307 (1995).

such phrases within the Directive, then Europeanized notions will be digested by judges in all fifteen member states in the application of provisions derived from the Directive. In theory at least, Article 177 cuts a direct channel of communication between national courts and the European Court and an indirect channel between national courts in different states, and through those channels flows a stream of developing European private law.

Contracts falling within the scope of application of the Directive

A definitional issue of major importance lies in the identification of the types of contract which are subjected to the controls envisaged by the Directive. The Directive covers contracts concluded between a seller or supplier and a consumer.[10] These terms are defined in Article 2 with reference to acting outside his trade, business or profession (consumer) and acting for purposes relating to his trade, business or profession, whether privately or publicly owned (seller or supplier).

The Recitals to the Directive clarify that this definition excludes, inter alia, employment contracts, contracts relating to succession rights, contracts relating to rights under family law and contracts relating to the incorporation and organization of companies or partnership agreements. However, it includes insurance contracts, although, as a result of the application of Article 4, the price of insurance as such does not fall to be checked against the required standard of fairness. It also includes oral contracts.

In so far as the Directive is based on an expectation that a risk of exploitation is inherent in contracts concluded between economically imbalanced parties, it can be criticized for an irrational limitation to contracts between consumers and traders. After all, similar problems may infect the relationship between large and small businesses. Indeed, the power differential between such parties may be a good deal wider than that between small trader and consumer. Some national systems accordingly govern business contracts, not simply consumer contracts, although typically through an appropriately modified regime. The EC

10. Article 1.

Directive is, admittedly, limited in its focus (although it does not preclude wider coverage under national law). At this stage of the development of European private law, where its very existence is neither universally accepted nor desired, it is perhaps necessary simply to acknowledge this restricted coverage, which cannot readily be defended on policy grounds. It should also not be neglected that the Directive's limitation to consumer contracts is explicable in the light of its roots in the EC consumer protection programme.

Terms falling within the scope of application of the Directive

The terms which are to be controlled require identification. Article 3 controls only contractual terms which have not been individually negotiated (although national law may go further in the scope of its coverage). This notion is explained further in Article 3(2). A term shall always be regarded as not individually negotiated (and therefore within the scope of the Directive) 'where it has been drafted in advance and the consumer has therefore not been able to influence the substance of the term, particularly in the context of a pre-formulated standard contract'. It rests with the seller or supplier who claims that a standard term has been individually negotiated to prove this.

The limitation to terms which have not been individually negotiated is more than simply a practical method of fixing the outer limit of potential legal intervention into the parties' bargain. It is of significance in an assessment of the underlying purpose of the Directive. Where the consumer has actually engaged in negotiation with the trader, it seems to be assumed that that process of negotiation acts as adequate protection from the risk of the imposition of unfair terms; or at least that the justification for legal intervention is lost. Only where negotiation is absent is intervention in the substance of the deal admitted. This is by no means uncontroversial. One might go so far as to adopt precisely the opposite perspective and argue that face-to-face discussion *deepens* the risk that an economically powerful trader will exploit the consumer. However, the Directive's limitation to terms that have not been individually negotiated demonstrates a suspicion of 'mass-produced' contracts, at least at the threshold of jurisdiction to check enforceability.

The use of plain, intelligible language

Article 5 provides that in the case of contracts where all or certain terms offered to the consumer are in writing, these terms must always be drafted in plain, intelligible language. Where there is doubt about the meaning of a term, the interpretation most favourable to the consumer shall prevail. This fits comfortably with the policy objective of securing transparency.

It will be recalled that Article 4 of the Directive provides that 'assessment of the unfair nature of the terms shall relate neither to the definition of the main subject matter of the contract nor to the adequacy of the price and remuneration, on the one hand, as against the services or goods supplies [sic] in exchange, on the other, *in so far as these terms are in plain intelligible language*'.[11] This is not an incursion into the principle that supervising the fairness of the price lies beyond the judicial function, but rather an assertion of the linkage between unfairness and intransparency.

Enforcement

Article 6 of the Directive requires member states to provide that unfair terms shall not bind the consumer. The contract shall continue to bind the parties if capable of remaining on foot without the unfair terms.

Article 7 provides that 'member states shall ensure that, in the interests of consumers and of competitors adequate and effective means exist to prevent the continued use of unfair terms in contracts concluded with consumers by sellers or suppliers'. It is further provided in Article 7(2) that the 'means' referred to shall include:

> provisions whereby persons or organisations, having a legitimate interest under national law in protecting consumers, may take action according to the national law concerned before the courts or before competent administrative bodies for a decision as to whether contractual terms drawn up for general use are unfair, so that they can apply appropriate and effective means to prevent the continued use of such terms.

[11.] My emphasis.

Article 7 is significant in its extension of enforcement mechanisms beyond litigation involving private parties[12] into the realms of public enforcement. However, it is far from clear precisely what is required by Article 7(2). Its rather unclear phrases may require subsequent elucidation of the nature of the enforcement obligation which is placed on member states. It is especially obscure whether member states are obliged to empower consumers' representative organizations to bring such proceedings as part of the general quest to secure the effective enforcement of EC law at national level, or whether such an obligation arises only where such organizations already enjoy privileged status under comparable national laws.

Minimum harmonization

As already mentioned, the Directive adheres to the technique of minimum harmonization in Article 8. This seems both desirable and necessary in the light of the prevailing diversity between national systems. It would be extremely difficult to establish a common Community rule apt to replace national rules, both for technical reasons of drafting and because of the risk that existing stricter national rules may be undermined. Although this diminishes the capacity of the Directive to create a level playing field for commercial actors, a Community minimum seems appropriate.

The choice of the minimum harmonization model demands that care be taken in implementation. Measures implementing the Directive will not simply pre-empt national law and become the sole source of legal control. The member states will be obliged to consider how best to incorporate the rules drawn from the Directive into their (in many cases) existing sophisticated regimes. It is already apparent that the desirable route of consolidation, yielding a single legal regime, has not been universally followed. This results in a fragmentation of consumer protection law within the national system.[13] Consumer protection law needs to be clear and simple if it is to be widely understood and used. Those states

---

12. Article 6.
13. On the UK position, see G. Howells and S. Weatherill, *Consumer Protection Law* (Aldershot, Dartmouth, 1995), ch. 9. More generally, see E. Hondius, 'The Reception of the Directive on Unfair Contract Terms by the Member States' 3 European Review of Private Law 241 (1995).

which have simply 'bolted on' measures implementing Directive 93/13 to their existing legal regimes diminish the practical utility of the whole system. It may be that the intransparency that results from taking the easy, 'bolt-on', option is a reason for doubting whether the obligation to implement the Directive in accordance with Articles 5 and 189 EC has been met.[14]

Directive 93/13 and 'European private law'

It would be an exaggeration to analyse the Directive as the cornerstone in the construction of a European private law. There are many obstacles to that process. The use of Article 177 to involve the European Court in the interpretation of the Directive and, in particular, phrases such as 'good faith', has an initial attraction in theory as a mechanism for bringing together national systems via the Directive. Yet one must concede that this process of convergence will be impeded by the probability that most cases involving the Directive will be relatively small-scale and litigants will have little incentive to seek a reference to Luxembourg, which involves notorious delay. More generally, the resistance of national legal cultures to 'Europeanization' of distinctive traditions of private law is of major significance.[15] Perhaps less often remarked upon is the potential resistance of the European Court to immersion in private law. Judges at the Court tend to be public lawyers or experts in international institutions by training. Requests for elucidation of notions such as good faith in Directive 93/13 may not be particularly welcome and may not find the Court in a mood to supply ambitious answers to Article 177 preliminary references. However, even such caveats cannot override the enormous *potential* of Directive 93/13 as a catalyst for gradual change of private law assumptions in Europe, although it is not the only such catalyst.[16]

---

14. F. Reynolds, Annotation, 110 LQR 1 (1994).
15. H. Collins, 'European Private Law and Cultural Identity of States' 3 European Review of Private Law 353 (1995); P. Legrand, 'European Legal Systems are not Converging' 45 ICLQ 52 (1996).
16. O. Lando, 'Principles of European Contract Law: An Alternative or a Precursor of European Legislation' *Rabels Zeitschrift* 261 (1992); J. Taupitz, *Europäische Privatrechtsvereinheitlichung heute und morgen* (Tübingen, JCB Mohr, 1993); A. Hartkamp *et al* (eds), *Towards a European Civil Code* (Dordrecht, Martinus Nijhoff, 1994).

A particularly remarkable aspect of the Directive is the assertion in the Preamble that the measure may encourage cross-border shoppers. It is explained that an absence of common rules of consumer protection impedes cross-border movement *by consumers* because of their ignorance of rules prevailing elsewhere than in their home state. So a common rule encourages cross-border movement. This represents an intriguing focus on consumer, not trader, mobility as an element in the process of market integration. Indeed, the logic could be used to support proposals advanced under Article 100a EC, and respecting Article 100a(3), to harmonize *all* private law, in so far as it differs state by state! Politically, this is not at present feasible, but there is a growing interest in – and in some quarters a corresponding disquiet about – the emerging contours of a European private law. It is of potentially prime importance to the future shaping of EC consumer policy that the inducement of consumer mobility is seen as a key element in the realization of an integrated market. The consumer is not merely a passive beneficiary.

The Green Paper on consumer guarantees

The Commission has not reached the limits of its current ambitions to assert an EC law intervention into national contract law. In November 1993 it published a Green Paper on 'Guarantees for Consumer Goods and After-Sales Service'.[17] Benefiting the consumer through improved transparency is a major objective of the Green Paper, but, like the Directive on Unfair Terms in Consumer Contracts, it also envisages regulation of the substance of the transaction. In fact, whereas Directive 93/13 envisages a 'negative' control of unfair terms, in the sense that it renders terms unenforceable, the Green Paper on guarantees tends towards a positive intervention by inserting a basic protective term into consumer contracts.

There are two types of guarantee considered by the Commission in the Green Paper: the legal guarantee and the commercial guarantee.

The legal guarantee is the minimum level of contractual warranty set by law, typically covering matters such as the

17. Com (93) 509.

quality of a product. Such legal minima offer the consumer a basic legal protection which is independent of any negotiated terms. The rules vary state by state.

The commercial guarantee is that promised as a result of negotiation between the parties. It might, for example, cover a promise that the product will be repaired if it breaks within a certain period. The commercial guarantee amounts to a private contractual arrangement.

The Green Paper is motivated by a policy which is close to that which informs Directive 93/13. It is driven by the perception that the development of common Community consumer protection rules can serve as a means of breeding the consumer confidence in integration which is indispensable to the realization of the internal market. The Green Paper asserts that 'Cross-border shopping can only flourish if the consumer knows he will enjoy the same guarantee and after-sales service conditions no matter where the supplier is located'.[18] Accordingly, the Green Paper envisages the establishment of a minimum level of protection which consumers will enjoy, irrespective of the country in which they shop. It airs suggestions for the creation of a Community framework within which the guarantees may operate.

The Green Paper suggests there should be a Community legal guarantee. This would act as a minimum, above which member states could add further protection. The advantage would lie in the security enjoyed by the cross-border consumer that, at the very least, protection under the guarantee would be available wherever a purchase takes place. The Community guarantee would thus play a part in inducing consumers to treat the market as integrated.

The Green Paper includes a summary of existing national practice as background to its suggested framework of Community law. Drawing on national experience, the proposed guarantee would apply to the sale of movable consumer goods that are durable and new. The desirability of extension to the services sector is not examined in any depth. The Commission is undecided whether to add a requirement relating to the status of the parties, which would limit the guarantee to deals between traders and consumers. The Green Paper suggests a guarantee

18. Page 5.

based on the 'failure to meet the consumer's legitimate expectation'. The guarantee would be enforceable against both vendor and manufacturer; and enforceable by consumer and subsequent owners. It would, accordingly, operate beyond the strict confines of the contractual chain. In order to protect the consumer from pressure and potential exploitation, it is proposed that the guarantee could not be waived by private agreement.

The perceived problem with the commercial guarantee is the absence of legal framework. The nature of commercial guarantees varies enormously, state by state, sector by sector. Where there are fifteen different systems of legal guarantee in the EC, there are thousands of different commercial guarantee. This is liable to render the market intransparent. The Commission's preferred response is for a mandatory legal framework applicable to all commercial guarantees, plus an optional 'European Guarantee'. The mandatory legal framework would involve enforceability of commercial guarantees up and down the distribution chain, in line with suggestions made as regards the legal guarantee. The European Guarantee would provide a framework which traders may choose to adopt. It would include the application of standard guarantee conditions in all the member states for the same type of goods of the same brand.

Since the Green Paper on consumer guarantees

The tentatively expressed ideas of the Green Paper would, if pursued, represent a further plank in the construction of a European private law. After the publication of the Green Paper in November 1993, the Commission embarked on an intensive round of consultation. Reaction was mixed. The Green Paper left open the precise form which Community intervention in the field might take. It seems implicit that a Community legal guarantee would be effective as a means of buttressing consumer confidence only if it is adopted by way of Directive under Article 100a, on the model of the Directive on unfair terms in consumer contracts. In the light of legal diversity and driven by the fear of impairing existing protection, one would anticipate the incorporation of the minimum harmonization formula. However, a formal proposal along these lines has not been put forward, and political will is not evidently strong. The commercial guarantee may be more susceptible to adoption, at least initially, as a soft law instrument, offering traders a model into which they may opt. Article 129a(1)(b) might provide a suitable legal base for these purposes. However, development here, too, has been slow. European private law, welcome or not, will be no overnight phenomenon.

CHAPTER FIVE

Product liability

The Product Liability Directive

Directive 85/374 harmonizes laws concerning liability for defective products.[1] It is commonly referred to as the 'Product Liability Directive'. Strictly, it is a measure adopted in order to advance the integration of the market. Its Treaty base is Article 100. Harmonization of national provisions concerning the liability of the producer for damage caused by defectiveness of products is required in the light of the distortions in competition in the Community and the impact on the movement of goods which are caused by divergences between the laws of the different member states. However, the harmonization of laws governing liability for defective products has a profound impact on the position of the consumer. Accordingly, Directive 85/374 is a major measure of Community consumer protection policy, albeit, in strict constitutional terms, as an incidental consequence of its principal objective.

The first Commission proposal in the field of product liability appeared in 1976.[2] The fact that it took nine years thereafter to achieve agreement on the Directive indicates the depth of controversy which surrounded this initiative. National systems of tort law vary, especially in their choice of the criteria according to which shall be judged the liability of the supplier to an injured consumer.[3] Aspects of the debate are reflected in the text of the Directive that was finally adopted. In several areas the mark of

---

[1.] OJ 1985 L210/29.   [2.] OJ 1976 C241/9.
[3.] P. Kelly and R. Attree, *European Product Liability* (London, Butterworths, 1992); G. Howells, *Comparative Product Liability* (Aldershot, Dartmouth, 1992).

uncomfortable compromise is unmistakable. In particular, a small number of options is permitted to member states, which detracts from the uniformity of the rules which are to be implemented. In fact, this Directive is a perfect case study of the problems which confront the Community legislature when it attempts to drive the policy of internal market building deep into the heartland of national private law.

The harmonized liability regime under the Directive

If one begins with an appreciation that divergence between national rules governing liability for the supply of defective products hinders market integration, then one's concern focuses on the need to establish a common rule and not on the content of that rule. Theoretically, the objective of harmonization will be achieved by setting the liability threshold at any level, provided only that it operates at a uniform level throughout the Community. And the Product Liability Directive was adopted under Article 100, before the Single European Act inserted, inter alia, Article 100a(3) into the Treaty, which for all its imperfections at least ensured an association of sorts between internal market policy and high levels of consumer protection.[4] However, the basis of the harmonized regime established by the Directive is liability without fault on the part of the producer of a defective product. Such a system of 'strict' liability, in contrast to fault-based liability, is considerably to the advantage of a consumer who has suffered loss. The Recitals to the Directive justify the choice of a harmonized system founded on liability without fault with reference to 'the fair apportionment of the risks inherent in modern technological production'. More fully, one would explain the allocation to the producer of the risk of defectiveness as efficient and fair in the light of the producer's capacity to buy insurance against loss and thereby to spread the costs of compensating a small number of injured consumers amongst all purchasers by reflecting insurance costs in a slightly higher price. Fault-based liability systems typically leave the consumer injured in the absence of fault without redress, which

---

4. Chapter 1, p. 17.

attracts criticism for its inequitable allocation of risk. Moreover, the difficulty and cost of showing fault in private litigation often deters a consumer from pursuing a claim even where there are chances of success. Accordingly, the influence of consumer protection is felt in the structure of this Directive. It has been drafted in part with reference to the need to secure effective consumer protection, despite its formal legal basis under Article 100 as a measure of market integration.

The core of the Directive is found in Article 1, which declares that 'The producer shall be liable for damage caused by a defect in his product'. This is a dramatically strong pro-consumer statement of risk allocation. On its face, the Directive is a remarkable piece of legislation, which seems to cut deep into national private law. Article 1 raises several definitional issues which are addressed in the succeeding Articles of the Directive.

Products covered by the Directive

By virtue of Article 2, those products covered by the Directive comprise all movables with the exception of primary agricultural products – other than those which have undergone initial processing – and game. The precise meaning of the notion of the qualifying phrase 'industrial processing' must await judicial clarification.

Article 15(1)(a) permits states to opt to bring primary agricultural products and game within the scope of the Directive. This is an option which detracts from the uniformity of the regime envisaged by the Directive. The initial exclusion of these products, which may certainly cause harm to the consumer, is readily attributable to the power of the farming lobby in Europe.

Persons liable under the Directive

The liability of a 'producer' covers the manufacturer of a finished product, the producer of any raw material or the manufacturer of a component part.[5] This embraces a wide range of persons, from the single craftsman or -woman to the large multinational

5. Article 3.

enterprise. Moreover, it extends to persons presenting themselves as producers, by, for example, affixing their name or trade mark to the item. This would catch the supermarket which chooses to apply its own brand name to a product. Such a marketing strategy converts the supermarket into a producer for the purposes of the Directive. Article 3(2) brings the importer of a product into the Community within the scope of liability as a producer for these purposes.

A supplier may incur liability for the supply of a defective product, although under Article 3(3) the supplier is able to escape liability by identifying the producer or his or her own supplier. In the light of this provision, commercial prudence dictates that suppliers of products should maintain careful records of the source of goods which they supply. Without such records, the buck will stop with them. From the perspective of the consumer, this system ensures that a claim for compensation cannot be defeated by an initial inability to identify the original producer, provided a supplier can be identified. The claim can be pursued against the supplier or against a party further up the chain identified by the supplier. However, contributory neglience by the consumer may operate to reduce an award in accordance with Article 8(2) of the Directive.

Article 7(c) provides that a producer is not liable as a result of the Directive where it is proved that 'the product was neither manufactured by him for sale or any form of distribution for economic purpose nor manufactured or distributed by him in the course of his business'. This frees the person who cooks for guests at a private dinner party from liability should the food prepared be defective.

The notion of 'defectiveness'

The key notion of 'defectiveness', which is a condition of liability in Article 1, is elaborated in Article 6, which states that a product is defective where it does not provide the safety which a person is entitled to expect. Expectation is to be judged with reference to all the circumstances; a non-exhaustive list is supplied in Article 6(1). The list includes reference to '[t]he use to which it could reasonably be expected that the product would be put', which indicates that a product may be defective where it causes damage as a result of foreseeable *mis*use. The insistence of Article 6(2) that a product is not to be considered defective solely because a better product is subsequently put into circulation demonstrates that the product must achieve a relative level of safety, not an absolute level. The fundamental issue arising under Article 6 of the Directive is that it ensures that the focus is on the condition of the product, whereas, by contrast, a fault-based system looks to the conduct of the producer.

The 'development risk' defence

The system of strict liability on which the Directive appears to be based is diluted by the inclusion of a so-called 'development risk' defence in Article 7(e). A producer of a defective product is able to escape liability by proving 'that the state of scientific and technical knowledge at the time when he put the product into circulation was not such as to enable the existence of the defect to be discovered'.

The producer of a product which is, with hindsight, indubitably defective does not incur liability if able to show the flaw to be, loosely interpreted, unknown and unknowable. In such circumstances the allocation of risk is shifted back on to the shoulders of the unlucky consumer.

The precise nature of this defence awaits judicial elaboration. It is unclear how heavy the burden of proof on the producer will prove to be – what of a defect suspected but not strictly 'discovered'? or the defect in, for example, a drug which has been publicized by one scientist only in an obscure journal in a minor language? or even identified by one scientist but not publicized at all?[6] One can argue cogently that Articles 1 and 7(e) of the Directive are irreconcilable, in that the apparent focus on the defective condition of the product within Article 1 is at odds with the reassertion of patterns of producer knowledge in Article 7(e). It may emerge that the combination of Articles 1 and 7(e) of the Directive do little more than assert an essentially fault-based liability regime, albeit with a burden cast on the producer to show the absence of fault, rather than on the consumer to show

6. C. Newdick, 'The Development Risk Defence of the Consumer Protection Act 1987' Cambridge Law Journal 455 (1988).

its presence.[7] The matter may be aired before the European Court in infringement proceedings initiated against the UK, which has chosen to implement the Directive in such a way as to make plain its belief that the defence acts as a potentially significant protection for the (loosely stated) 'non-negligent' producer.[8]

Given these complexities, one may naturally wonder why the development risk defence was included in the Directive at all. A rationale for this producer-friendly development risk defence lies in the perception that, in the absence of such a defence, producers would have had a greatly diminished incentive to invest in new products, not least because of problems in securing insurance cover under a system of 'pure' strict liability. Accordingly, during the negotiation of the Directive, proponents of the development risk defence, such as the government of the UK, emphasized its role in sustaining incentives to pursue technological innovation, which is, in the long run, to the advantage of the consumer and of society generally. North American evidence of the damage done by rising awards, leading to an upwards spiral in insurance costs, was commonly cited. None the less, this view was unacceptable to several member states, who regarded such protection for the producer as incompatible with a vigorous consumer policy. North American evidence was, for many observers, at best equivocal and at worst irrelevant to the very different legal and commercial conditions prevailing in Europe.[9] The disagreement was resolvable only through a compromise, which wrecked the uniformity of application of the Directive on this particular point. Article 15(1)(b) permits member states the option of extending liability even to defects of this type. So in some states the 'development risk' defence will be available to traders faced with claims by consumers harmed by the supply of defective products, but in

---

7. C. Newdick, 'Risk, Uncertainty and Knowledge in the Development Risks Defence' 20 Anglo-Am LRev 309 (1991).

8. Case C-300/95 *Commission v United Kingdom*: the UK has implemented Art. 7(e) in s 4(1)(e) of the Consumer Protection Act 1987 so that it is a defence for the producer to show '. . . that the state of scientific and technical knowledge at the relevant time was not such that a producer of products of the same description as the product in question might be expected to have discovered the defect if it had existed in his products while they were under his control'.

9. See discussion by M. Shapo in 'Comparing Products Liability: Concepts in European and American Law' 26 Cornell International Law Journal 279 (1993).

other states, where different choices have been made, no such protection can be relied on.[10]

The Directive and a European tort law

The sceptical observer may readily be forgiven for doubting the value of EC intervention. Given the inclusion in the Directive of options, what price effective harmonization? The development risk option, in particular, has attracted criticism for its capacity to induce forum shopping by consumers (who will prefer to sue in states which have opted to exclude the defence); and to distort business choices about where to locate (there may even be a preference to 'test' products in states which maintain the defence). Certainly, the Directive offers scope for an enhanced level of consumer protection in the Community, especially in those countries, such as the UK, previously wedded to a fault-based liability system. Yet the development risk defence undermines even this advance. The inclusion of the defence in national implementing measures is not mandatory, but one would anticipate that few states would choose to reject it, given that such a step would place 'their' firms at a competitive disadvantage in comparison with firms in neighbouring states. This has proved accurate; the defence has been widely, though not universally, accepted.[11] The Directive was hailed at the time of its adoption as a step towards the Europeanization of private law. Article 1, in particular, seems to involve an ambitious assertion of a European standard for product liability, and invites the European Court, fed by Article 177 references, to shape European notions of defectiveness.[12] Yet no case has ever been referred to the European Court under Article 177 in connection with the interpretation of the Directive. In fact, there have been relatively few reported decisions before national courts. This by

10. C. J. S. Hodges, *Product Liability: European Laws and Practice* (London, Sweet and Maxwell, 1993).
11. Annex, COM (95) 617, First Report on the Application of the Directive. See also T. Bourgoignie, 'The 1985 Council Directive on product liability and its implementation in the member states of the European Union' in M. Goyens (ed.), *Directive 85/374/EEC on product liability: ten years after* (Louvain-la-Neuve, Centre de Droit de la Consommation, 1996).
12. Cf. G. Howells, 'Product Liability' in A. Hartkamp *et al* (eds), *Towards a European Civil Code* (Dordrecht, Martinus Nijhoff, 1994).

no means constitutes conclusive proof that the Directive's impact has been slight, for it is conceivable that, for example, the existence of the Directive may have prompted informal settlements (typically by insurance companies) in favour of the consumer in circumstances which previously would have left the consumer without a remedy in law or practice.[13] Moreover, cases involving personal injury, complicated by issues of causation mixed with assessment of defectiveness, may take several years to reach full trial. In sum, the impact of the Directive remains difficult to measure.

Choice of liability rules engages a host of distinct, often competing, conceptions about the function of the private law in regulating the economy in particular and society generally.[14] Community intervention in the field is driven explicitly by the process of market integration. It becomes difficult for the Community to reflect the range of interests underpinning national systems in a harmonized rule. This, in turn, causes the harmonization measure to burst. In order to secure political agreement, a common rule must be adjusted to include options which contradict the notion of a common pattern.

It remains contentious how far options granted in Directives constitute an acceptable recognition of national peculiarities and how far they undermine the whole notion of the level playing field within the Community. It is politically realistic to suppose that complete unanimity is frequently neither feasible nor, perhaps, desirable, but a Directive which is pitted with options may simply conceal fundamental disagreement which it was judged politically expedient to conceal with a well-nigh worthless legislative product.

The 1995 review of the Directive

Part of the compromise struck at the time of the Directive's adoption finds expression in Article 15(3). This provides that in 1995 the Commission shall report on the operation of the development risk defence and the optional exclusion of it. The

---

13. M. Mildred, 'The Impact of the Directive in the United Kingdom', in Goyens, *Directive 85/374/EEC on product liability: ten years after.*
14. J. Stapleton, *Product Liability* (London, Butterworths, 1994).

Council shall consider whether to repeal Article 7(e), which would strip producers of protection from liability for loss caused by unknown and unknowable defects. On the one hand, this review was a convenient device for avoiding final decisions on controversial issues as part of the compromise necessary to achieve the adoption of this important Directive in 1985. On the other hand, it offered an opportunity to use the Directive's first years constructively as a test period at the end of which more informed assessment of its contribution could be attempted. In the event, the report on the application of the Directive, which was published in late 1995, is a profoundly uninspiring document.[15] It contains just one page of comment. The Commission observes that the Directive has eased the burden on the plaintiff, but that it does not appear to have caused an increase in the number of claims brought, nor in level of insurance premiums payable. The Commission confesses that 'experience is still limited' and that, accordingly, it does not intend to submit proposals for amendment of the Directive. It will continue to monitor developments. This does not refute the notion that harmonization is a gradual process, based on experience accumulated over time, but it serves as a reminder that the process may be extremely slow.

Liability for the supply of defective services

It is natural to speculate whether the liability system for supply of defective goods introduced in 1985 by the Product Liability Directive could profitably be extended into the field of liability for the supply of defective services. The Commission decided to test the water in 1990 by publishing a draft Directive on the liability of suppliers of services.[16]

In some respects, the draft was designed to complement the Product Liability Directive, although there were differences between the two regimes. The core of the draft Directive's proposal for a common regime was contained in Article 1:

> The supplier of a service shall be liable for damage to the health and physical integrity of persons or the physical integrity of

15. COM (95) 617.   16. COM (90) 482.

movable or immovable property, including the persons or property which were the object of the service, caused by a fault committed by him in the performance of the service.

This appears to impose fault-based liability, and is thus quite distinct from the approach taken in Article 1 of the Product Liability Directive. However, the proposal qualified this position significantly by providing that the supplier must prove the absence of fault. This would offer practical advantages to the consumer claimant. However, the nature of the proposed regime would be affected by the requirement that '[i]n assessing the fault, account shall be taken of the behaviour of the supplier of the service, who, in normal and reasonably foreseeable conditions, shall ensure the safety which may reasonably be expected'.

In accordance with the use of Article 100a as the proposed legal base, the Commission presented the proposal with scrupulous care as an attempt not merely to protect the consumer, but primarily as an instrument designed to liberate trade by reducing uncertainty about insurance costs borne by suppliers operating in different states with different legal regimes. It was, however, plain even in 1990 that the draft Directive on liability of suppliers of services was released into a harsh, unyielding political environment. The draft was subjected to sustained criticism. The services industry, especially in its influential professional sector, lobbied hard against the initiative and little support was forthcoming among the member states. The draft appeared in the Commission's report submitted to the Edinburgh European Council in December 1992 in which the Commission reviewed existing and proposed legislation in the light of the subsidiarity principle.[17] The draft Directive on services liability featured on the list of measures which contained excessive detail and which were to be revised and drafted in a more general style.

It became plain that there was an absence of political will behind the proposed Directive. Eventually, a Communication from the Commission on new directions on the liability of suppliers of services was published in 1994.[18] The Commission concluded that its 'proposal stands no chance of being adopted without sweeping changes which would risk voiding it of much of its substance'. It therefore withdrew it. In the Communication

17. Chapter 1, pp. 33–4.   18. COM (94) 260.

on new directions, the Commission comments further that the specific circumstances of different services deserve greater consideration. The Commission 'will if necessary prepare draft texts concerning sectors in respect of which particular needs are established'.

It is not necessary simply to conclude that a political climate of suspicion about new Community initiatives of market regulation is solely to blame for this episode of thwarted ambition. Services are, after all, materially distinct in some respects from goods, particularly where they are intangible. The structure of a liability regime governing the supply of services may coherently differ from one affecting the supply of goods, as was indeed already envisaged in the Commission's original 1990 draft, based on a type of fault-based liability regime. However, it is hard to avoid the conclusion that the political climate of subsidiarity was, in this instance, fatal to the Commission's attempt to persuade a sufficient number of member states of the advisability of Community action in the field. A new pathway to the growth of a European tort law was therefore blocked.

CHAPTER SIX

Advertising law

Advertising and market integration

In modern marketing conditions, a successful commercial strategy involves more than offering a product or service for sale. Closely interwoven with the product or service is the advertising campaign which supports it. For new brands, in particular, it is scarcely conceivable that significant numbers of consumers will be induced to buy an unfamiliar product or service in the absence of investment in a strategy designed to draw consumers' attention to the qualities of the newcomer to the market. This is plainly of particular relevance to the process of European market integration. A traditional French product will be unlikely to make much headway into the German market, where it is unknown, unless accompanied by an advertising campaign and sustained by an effective distribution network. Advertising is a major feature of the modern market economy and it is indispensable in securing changes in existing market patterns.

Such introductory comments identify advertising as a method of consumer information and a basis for widening consumer choice. Adopting such a positive perspective, it should be encouraged; or at least not suppressed. Some of the case law discussed in Chapter 2 reflects this perception. In *GB-INNO v CCL*,[1] for example, a national law which prevented the provision of information to consumers by an advertiser was held incompatible with Article 30 as an unlawful obstacle to the free movement of goods. The impediment to an advertising technique affected the capacity of a cross-border trader to penetrate a new

[1.] Case C-362/88 [1990] ECR I-667.

market, thereby prejudicing consumer choice. In fact, cases dealing with advertising restrictions are emerging as among the most difficult to resolve in the light of the Court's ruling in *Keck and Mithouard*[2] which overturned earlier decisions and confined the scope of application of Article 30. Provided that the restriction on advertising affects all traders equally in law and in fact, the national measure appears to be immune from challenge based on Article 30. But where the measure prevents the out-of-state trader from constructing a strategy that will permit the realization of economies of scale within an integrating market, it requires justification against the standards recognized by Community law. This suggests a grey area between regulated aspects of advertising that can be separated from the strategy for selling the product or service, which fall beyond the scope of Article 30, and aspects of advertising which, by contrast, are sufficiently connected with the product or service to allow a challenge to national measures that restrict their use to be founded on Article 30. This is a difficult distinction to draw in the light of the modern marketing mix between product/service and its associated identity constructed through advertising.

Advertising takes many forms and not all deserve favourable appreciation. Advertising may mislead, advertising may offend. For some, advertising distorts consumer preference. National laws restrict advertising for a variety of reasons, differing state by state.[3] This has drawn the European Court into an assessment of the permissibility of types of national controls over advertising in so far as the required impediment to cross-border trade is shown. Whereas the restrictions in *GB-INNO* were ruled incompatible with Article 30, those in *Oosthoek*,[4] which prevented a strategy built around the offer of free gifts, were ruled lawful.[5] They served to protect the consumer from tactics that were liable to mislead and could, accordingly, be justified according to the standards of Community law, despite the restrictive effect on cross-border trade.

Beyond the Court's role in shaping a negative law approach to the permissibility of national advertising controls, the Community

---

[2.] Cases C-267 & 268/91 judgment of 24 November 1993, p. 42 above.
[3.] J. Maxeiner and P. Schotthöfer, *Advertising Law in Europe and North America* (Dordrecht, Kluwer, 1992).
[4.] Case 286/81 [1982] ECR 4575.   [5.] Chapter 2, p. 55.

itself has begun to put in place a pattern of positive law, regulating advertising at Community level. The constitutional rationale for these Community measures in the field of advertising has been the pursuit of market integration. Attention has focused on the use of Articles 100 and 100a as a basis for harmonizing national laws which have, as a result of disparity, impeded the development of integrated marketing strategies. However, it is a familiar theme of this book that, in putting in place common Community rules as a basis for integration, such harmonization measures also serve to (re)regulate the market according to Community standards.

So, in the early stages of the development of the Community, the legal regulation of advertising was the preserve of national authorities. Driven by the process of market integration, Community law has been obliged to develop an approach to advertising law.[6] This process was discussed in relation to the Court's perception in Chapter 2 and some of the requirements of information disclosure discussed in Chapter 3 impinge on advertising strategy. But the remainder of this chapter considers more direct legislative action in the field. Piecemeal though the Community strategy for controlling advertising techniques may be, the theme, here as elsewhere in the book, is that, notwithstanding the pre-Maastricht absence of an explicit Title in the Treaty dealing with consumer protection, a type of policy in the field has been unavoidably developed.

Misleading advertising

National laws controlling misleading advertising vary in their precise shape, but it is a relatively uncontroversial proposition that misleading advertising should be subject to regulatory control. *Mis*information of the consumer damages the effective operation of the competitive market system. This calls for intervention. This combination of circumstances led to the field of misleading advertising yielding the EC's first harmonization Directive in this area.

6. Cf. B. Schmitz, 'Advertising and Commercial Communications – Towards a Coherent and Effective EC Policy' 16 Journal of Consumer Policy 387 (1993); A. Vahrenwald, 'The Advertising Law of the EU' EIPR 279 (1996).

Directive 84/450 harmonizes national measures concerning misleading advertising.[7] It is based on Article 100. Variation between national laws in the field exerts a direct impact on the creation of a common market. The free circulation of goods and services is impeded by legislative disharmony. The familiar dual aim of EC measures affecting consumer protection is reflected in the Recitals to the Directive. It is asserted that misleading advertising may prejuduce consumers. Support for the need for a regulatory response is drawn from the second soft law programme for a consumer protection and information policy, agreed in 1981.[8] It is added that legal regulation of marketing practices is not simply an exercise in protecting the consumer. The establishment of common standards in this area also serves to protect business people whose fair commercial practices might be undermined by those engaged in misleading practices, to the overall detriment of the efficient operation of the market.

The meaning of 'misleading'

The key definition of 'misleading' for these purposes is addressed in Articles 2(2) and 3. Article 2(2) identifies the deceptive nature of the advertising as the key element. It is plainly appropriate to take a broad view of the surrounding circumstances in assessing the misleading nature of advertising. This is reflected in Article 3 of the Directive: 'Account shall be taken of all its features.' A non-exhaustive list in Article 3 refers to the characteristics of goods or services, price, conditions of supply and the nature and attributes of the advertiser.

The notion of misleading is plainly dependent on all the circumstances of the case. Nevertheless, it is capable of being interpreted by the European Court in the context of an Article 177 preliminary reference in the light of 'Europeanized' considerations. This is well illustrated by the Court's ruling in *Procureur de la République v X*.[9] The case reached the European Court as a preliminary reference from a French court dealing with an allegation of misleading advertising against a trader importing Nissan cars from Belgium for resale in France, where they were advertised as new cars available at lower prices than

---

7. OJ 1984 L250/17.   8. Chapter 1.   9. Case C-373/90 [1992] ECR I-131.

Nissan cars sold by the French exclusive distributor. The cars on offer were registered, but for importation purposes only. They had never been driven and were cheaper than French models because they possessed fewer accessories. Did this tactic secure a desirable widening of consumer choice, or did it create an unacceptable risk that the consumer would be misled into buying a model different from that which he or she expected to acquire? The French exclusive distributor lodged a complaint before the competent French court about the strategy. It was necessary to consider whether this amounted to misleading advertising within the meaning of the Directive, which should therefore be suppressed at national level. The European Court considered that 'It is when a car is first driven on the public highway, and not when it is registered, that it loses its character as a new car'. This made it plain that the imported cars should be regarded as new. The Court accepted that a national court might properly find advertising to be misleading where it seeks to conceal the fact that cars advertised as new were registered before importation and where knowledge of this would have deterred purchase by a *significant* number of consumers. The Court also considered that advertising cars as cheaper could only be misleading where a *significant* number of consumers were ignorant that the lower price was matched by the availability of fewer accessories. The Court concluded its relatively full reply to the questions referred to it by ruling that the Directive –

> must be interpreted as meaning that it does not preclude vehicles from being advertised as new, less expensive and guaranteed by the manufacturer when the vehicles concerned are registered solely for the purpose of importation, have never been on the road and are sold in a member state at a price lower than that charged by dealers established in that member state because they are equipped with fewer accessories.

The essence of the ruling is that the marketing of the cars could not be suppressed by the French authorities on the basis that it infringed the controls which the Directive required member states to put in place. This was not a case of misleading advertising.

The Court is plainly unreceptive to a broad reading of what may mislead. *Significant* levels of consumer confusion must be shown before the Directive's control is activated. The Court's choice of this relatively high threshold is probably motivated by concern to facilitate the commercial opportunities of a parallel importer in a sector which is notoriously marked by persisting fragmentation along national lines. Had the tactics employed by the dealer in Belgian cars been suppressed as misleading within the meaning of the Directive, then territorial protection within France would have been strengthened. It is plausible that the Court's interpretative approach to required levels of misapprehension among consumers took account of the ultimate consumer advantage that would flow from integration of the car market, yielding wider consumer choice. Advocate-General Tesauro was explicit in his observation that suppression of the type of advertising at stake 'would be likely in practice to hit parallel importers particularly hard'. The Court, too, chose to confirm this perspective, referring to the privileged position in Community law of parallel importers 'because they encourage trade and help reinforce competition'. So the chance of *some* consumer confusion was not adequate to treat the advertising practices as misleading within the meaning of the Directive. Underlying the ruling is an assumption that a sufficient majority of consumers is sufficiently well-informed to exercise a choice between different types of car. Here too Mr Tesauro was explicit: 'the average consumer, who I am convinced is not wholly undiscerning, is inclined . . . to make a careful comparison of the prices on offer and to enquire of the seller, sometimes very meticulously, about the accessories with which the vehicle is equipped.' This may be taken as a further illustration of the Court's use of the informed consumer as a lever to achieve market integration, in this instance occurring against the background of a Directive rather than the primary Treaty rules examined in Chapter 2. The consumer provided with the stipulated information cannot be regarded as misled.

Here, as in other circumstances, the issue centres on the delicate question of when beneficially wider choice in a more competitive market shades into prejudicially intransparent market conditions in which confusion, not choice, will greet the consumer.

Minimum harmonization

The Court's capacity to set the terms for parallel trade by restricting the possibilities for national action under the Directive is to some extent limited by Article 7 of the Directive. This is the minimum harmonization formula. It permits member states to set stricter rules than those contained in the Directive should they so wish. Those stricter rules must be compatible with the Treaty. In so far as they impede the free movement of goods they must comply with Articles 30–36. So, using the example of *Procureur de la République v X*, the Directive, as a minimum measure, would not prevent France adopting stricter laws controlling advertising, but it seems probable that such restrictions would be held incompatible with Article 30 EC. This was not made explicit by the Court, but it was the view expressed by the Commission in its submissions in *X*. Moreover, analogies with rulings such as *Rocher* and *Clinique*,[10] in which the Court found national restrictions on advertising to be unlawful, suggest that it would be difficult for stricter rules to be justified.

Enforcement

The practical impact of the Directive within national legal orders is naturally dependent on patterns of enforcement. The Directive is not content simply to leave it up to national authorities to choose how to implement the prohibition against misleading advertising. It makes specific reference to the type of institutional structures that must be established.

Article 4(1) obliges member states to 'ensure that adequate and effective means exist for the control of misleading advertising in the interests of consumers as well as competitors and the general public'. Legal provisions shall enable persons or organizations, regarded under national law as having a legitimate interest in prohibiting misleading advertising, to pursue one or both of two stipulated routes: first, the taking of legal action against such advertising; second, the bringing of such advertising before an administrative authority competent either to decide on complaints or to initiate appropriate legal proceedings. Article 4(2) requires courts and administrative authorities to be empowered to take stipulated forms of action, including the making of cessation orders, in the event of offending advertising.

---

10. Case C-126/91 judgment of 18 May 1993 and Case C-315/92 [1994] ECR I-317, examined in Chapter 2.

The policy which underpins this structure is directed at the perceived need to permit states the option of retaining administrative structures as adequate regulation in the area. The UK, in particular, was concerned to avoid the imposition of a judicial structure. It was also unwilling to see the exclusion of its self-regulatory structure, which the government viewed as satisfactory. Article 4(3) of the Directive requires that, where the administrative option is taken, the authorities shall be, inter alia, impartial (therefore, not dominated by advertisers) and that, where the powers are the exclusive preserve of the administrative authority, decisions shall be reasoned and shall be subject to judicial review in the event of impropriety or unreasonableness. Article 5 emphasizes the receptivity of the structure to extra-legal enforcement. Article 5 makes it clear that voluntary control of misleading advertising by self-regulatory bodies is not excluded, although proceedings of this nature must be additional to, not in substitution for, the court or administrative route established by Article 4.

The Directive does not explicitly require that standing be conferred on consumer organizations to challenge misleading advertising before either courts or administrative agencies. It goes no further than ensuring that such organizations have the possibility of making a complaint about misleading advertising. States are then required to provide 'adequate and effective' means of control in accordance with the Directive. Some states have chosen to provide consumer organizations with standing to initiate judicial proceedings, but others, including the UK, have done no more than offer such organizations the opportunity to lodge complaints with the relevant administrative body (the Director General of Fair Trading in the UK).

Comparative advertising

The Commission first devoted attention to the possibility of legislative harmonization in the field of advertising regulation in the late 1970s. The original draft proposal in this area covered misleading, unfair and comparative advertising.[11] The first two types of advertising were to be controlled, the third, comparative,

11. OJ 1978 C70/4, amended proposal OJ 1979 C194/3.

was to be liberalized. However, the Directive as finally adopted, discussed above, excludes provisions concerning unfair and comparative advertising, and deals only with control of misleading advertising. This reflects the difficulties of achieving a satisfactory harmonized regime against a background of legal heterogeneity.[12] In particular, although the notion of unfair advertising as an aspect of unfair competition between traders is relatively well understood in several continental European systems, English law recognizes no developed notion of a law against unfair competition.[13] Differences in legal tradition similarly explain the exclusion of comparative advertising. This technique is tightly controlled in several member states, including Germany, as an aspect of unfair competition, whereas it is largely seen as unexceptionable in other states, including the UK, where a liberal attitude is taken other than with regard to trade-mark infringement.

The Commission has persisted in its attempts to add Directives on comparative and unfair advertising to that agreed in 1984 on misleading advertising. In June 1991 it proposed a Council Directive concerning comparative advertising which would have amended and extended Directive 84/450.[14] However, legislative proposals do not exist in isolation from evolution in other areas of Community law. National restrictions on comparative advertising were not immune from decisions of the European Court on the scope of application of Article 30. This proved to be a route towards liberalization even in the absence of legislative action. In *GB-INNO-BM v CCL*, discussed in Chapter 2, restrictions on comparative advertising imposed in Luxembourg were shown to be incompatible with Article 30 because of their inhibition on the free circulation of products capable of being marketed with the support of such techniques. The Commission made explicit reference to this ruling in its June 1991 proposal. In view of the challenge to national laws that control comparative advertising which is presented by Article 30 in the wake of the ruling in *GB-INNO v CCL*, the need to liberalize comparative

---

12. B. Ludwig, *Irreführende und vergleichende Werbung in der EG* (Baden-Baden, Nomos, 1995).

13. Cf. G. Schricker, 'European Harmonization of Unfair Competition Law – a Futile Venture?' in *International Review of Industrial Property and Copyright Law* 6/1991, 788 (1991).

14. OJ 1991 C180/1.

advertising by introducing positive Community law is diminished. The Commission's proposed Directive was designed largely to permit comparative advertising, subject to qualifications which are principally directed to ensuring the fairness of the comparison. Such liberalization is designed to enhance consumer information and to stimulate competition.

Adoption in Council was not secured and the Commission published an amended proposal in 1994.[15] In the interim, the subsidiarity principle gained prominence in the political atmosphere surrounding existing and proposed Community legislative activity.[16] The Commission declared that it had reviewed the proposal on comparative advertising in the light of the demands of the subsidiarity principle. Nevertheless, the thrust in favour of controlled liberalization of the practice of comparative advertising was maintained and the adjustments to the original proposal were relatively modest. The measure has not yet been formally adopted.

Tobacco advertising

Tobacco advertising has been increasingly the subject of control in most member states in response to the growing awareness of the health risks for both smokers and non-smokers associated with tobacco consumption. In line with much of the legislative activity surveyed in this book, the diversity of regulatory responses provides a ready rationale for Community legislative intervention in the field based on Article 100a.

Directive 89/622 concerns the labelling of tobacco products and it takes Article 100a as its legal base.[17] The Directive was adopted in November 1989 by qualified majority vote in Council, which is the requirement under Article 100a. The UK, which has preferred to employ a voluntary approach in this sector in the past, voted in vain against the measure.

Directive 89/622 provides that products shall carry a general warning, which in English shall read 'Tobacco seriously damages health'. Furthermore, manufacturers are required to select from a list of additional warnings which have to be printed on packets of cigarettes. The Directive stipulates that the warnings shall

15. OJ 1994 C136/4.   16. Chapter 1.   17. OJ 1989 L359/1.

112

cover at least four per cent of the relevant surface area.[18] Directive 89/622 was amended by Directive 92/41, which is also based on Article 100a.[19] The additional warnings must be applied to all tobacco products, not just cigarettes. Moreover, a prohibition was imposed on certain tobacco products for oral use.

The Commission has maintained the view that the scope of Community action in the field should be extended. A proposal for a further Directive was issued in 1991, which envisaged the introduction of a complete ban on advertising, save within tobacco retail outlets.[20] This proposal, like its two predecessors, was based on Article 100a. The approval of the Parliament was received in February 1992, although the Parliament suggested amendments which would have rendered the controls still more rigorous. The Commission then redrafted its proposal to accommodate some of these amendments and issued a fresh proposal in April 1992.[21]

However, at this point it proved impossible to secure an adequate majority in Council to secure the adoption of a third Community measure governing the legal regulation of tobacco advertising. A number of member states were opposed to the 1992 initiative, and subsequently a sufficient number has remained opposed to prevent the assembly of the support required in Council to adopt the measure by qualified majority vote. Given the economic significance of the tobacco industry, it is no surprise that these proposals have attracted fierce and sustained opposition.

In the absence of the necessary political will in Council, the Commission's proposal stands no chance of becoming law. Further speculation on its merits and its constitutionality is of no immediate practical importance. However, even were the required number of states to be won round to the Commission's view that such a Directive is of value, there might still arise significant arguments against the Community's competence to adopt such a measure at all or, at least, to adopt it on the basis of Article 100a. These are aspects of the debate that deserve brief summary,

---

18. States must admit on to their market imported packets which carry a warning covering four per cent of surface area, but they remain free to impose stricter rules on home production; Case C-11/92 *R v Secretary of State, ex parte Gallaher Ltd* judgment on 22 June 1993.
19. OJ 1992 L158.   20. OJ 1991 C167/3.   21. OJ 1992 C129/5.

for they are of relevance beyond the sector of tobacco advertising.

Article 100a empowers the Community to adopt measures to eliminate differences between national measures, but it has been objected that action of the type proposed in 1991, involving a complete ban with only limited exceptions, reaches beyond the objective of market integration and pursues instead the objective of health protection, in respect of which the Community lacked competence prior to the Maastricht amendments. The Commission has maintained the view that Article 100a is an appropriate base for its proposal, notwithstanding its extended scope, insisting on the contribution it would make to the elimination of the trade distortive effect of different national laws in the field in the light of the reference to a high level of health protection found in Article 100a(3). It has also added reference to relevant soft law – the 1986 Council Resolution on an EC programme of action against cancer.[22] Choice of legal base must be made according to objective factors amenable to judicial review, and it would ultimately fall to the Court to determine whether an interventionist measure of the type proposed by the Commission could validly be made under the internal market base, Article 100a. If it could *not*, then a measure based on Article 100a would be invalid even where supported by adequate political will to achieve a QMV in Council. There would then arise a need to search for an appropriate base. The Treaty on European Union inserted Article 129, a new Title on Public Health, into the EC Treaty, but that provision does not envisage harmonization of laws. It might be possible to employ Article 235 in such circumstances, if it is shown that adequate powers are not available elsewhere in the Treaty, but Article 235 would be of little practical utility as a base for the adoption of hotly contested proposals, for Article 235 requires unanimity in Council.

A separate source of challenge to the validity of a measure of the type proposed in 1991 by the Commission on tobacco advertising may be found in the general principles of Community law. Specifically, it is feasible that it might be ruled incompatible with notions of freedom of expression for the Community to introduce a legislative ban on advertising. This notion of 'commercial free speech', whereby traders assert a constitutional

22. OJ 1986 C184/19.

right to challenge legislative inhibition on their freedom, is relatively undeveloped in Europe, although it has a longer pedigree in North America.[23]

In *ERT v Dimotiki* the Court interpreted the scope of the freedom to provide services 'in the light of the general principle of freedom of expression embodied in Article 10 of the European Convention on Human Rights'.[24] In that case state restrictions on broadcasting had to be justified with reference to the European Convention, which is not formally part of EC law, but which is fed into the fabric of the general principles of Community law by the European Court. No adequate justification for the restrictions was forthcoming. The general principles of Community law apply both to national authorities – in so far as they act within the scope of application of Community law, which was the situation in *ERT v Dimotiki* – and to Community institutions. It is, accordingly, appropriate to check the validity of, inter alia, legislative action by the Community which affects commercial free speech against these standards.

It is by no means suggested here that advertising restrictions which are tested against laws pertaining to freedom of expression would or should be necessarily invalidated.[25] It is properly recognized in Article 10(2) of the European Convention that public authorities are entitled to exercise some degree of control in accordance with what is 'necessary in a democratic society'.[26] In so far as rights to freedom of expression are transplanted from the Convention to EC law, then they are accompanied by legal recognition that such rights are not absolute. However, the commercially sensitive identification of the permissible scope of control is liable to generate litigation should the Commission succeed in its quest to persuade a sufficient number of member states to agree to further controls over tobacco advertising.[27]

23. A. M. Collins, 'Commercial Speech and the Free Movement of Goods and Services at Community Law', in J. O'Reilly (ed.), *Human Rights and Constitutional Law* (Dublin, Butterworths, 1992); W. Skouris (ed.), *Advertising and Constitutional Rights in Europe* (Baden-Baden, Nomos, 1994).

24. Case C-260/89 [1991] ECR I-2925.

25. Cf. A. Hutchinson, 'Money Talk: Against Constitutionalizing (Commercial) Speech' 17 Canadian Business Law Journal 2 (1990).

26. No violation of Art. 10 of the Convention was found in *Markt Intern and Beerman v Germany* ECHR Series A No. 165, judgment of 20 November 1989.

27. The ability of tobacco producers themselves to pursue such challenge before the European Court would be hampered by the relatively strict restrictions on standing in Art. 173 EC.

Television broadcasting

Directive 89/552 harmonizes national laws concerning the pursuit of television broadcasting activities.[28] Its legal base is Articles 57(2) and 66 EC and its primary purpose is the removal of obstacles to free movement of television broadcasting services within the Community. Laws differ between member states and thereby act as impediments to trade. The Directive lays down the minimum rules needed to guarantee freedom of transmission. The structure of the Directive provides that the originating state then bears responsibility for ensuring that the broadcasts are in conformity with the law and that secondary control in the receiving state shall normally not be imposed.

Chapter IV of the Directive, comprising Articles 10–21, is entitled 'Television advertising and sponsorship'. From the point of view of the consumer, the most significant provisions of the Directive are those directed at the control of advertisements for tobacco, medical products and alcoholic beverages.

Article 13 prohibits 'all forms of television advertising for cigarettes and other tobacco products'. Article 14 prohibits 'television advertising for medicinal products and medical treatment available only on prescription in the member state within whose jurisdiction the broadcaster falls'. Sponsorship of programmes by traders in these fields is prohibited under Article 17(2) of the Directive.

Article 15 adopts a more nuanced approach to advertisements for alcoholic beverages. There is no outright prohibition, but the Directive controls such advertising through a list of six criteria with which advertising shall comply. Article 16 is directed at the protection of minors from advertisements. Chapter V of the Directive (Article 22) deals with this matter in the context of broadcasting generally.

As in the case of tobacco advertising, here too arise questions about constitutional limitations that may be imposed on the capacity of the Community legislature to restrict advertising. Indeed, the broadcasting industry provided the background to the ruling in *ERT v Dimotiki*, mentioned above. Community legislative activity in the field of broadcasting clearly recognizes the connection with the principles of the European Convention.

[28.] OJ 1989 L298/23.

The Preamble to Directive 89/552 on television broadcasting declares that:

> Whereas this right as applied to the broadcasting and distribution of television services is also a specific manifestation in Community law of a more general principle, namely the freedom of expression as enshrined in Article 10(1) of the Convention for the Protection of Human Rights and Fundamental Freedoms ratified by all member states; whereas for this reason the issuing of Directives on the broadcasting and distribution of television programmes must ensure their free movement in the light of the said Article and subject only to the limits set by paragraph 2 of that Article and by Article 56(1) of the Treaty.

Naturally, such an assertion cannot amount to conclusive evidence that the restrictions on advertising envisaged by the Directive do not infringe rights to freedom of expression. Such matters may yet be brought before the Court. However, it is plain that Community regulation of advertising is developing in the shadow of two European legal orders, that of the EC and that of the European Convention. The growing significance of these issues prompted the Commission to issue a Green Paper on 'Commercial Communications in the Internal Market' in 1996,[29] which discusses issues of both market integration and freedom of expression. The Commission observes that cross-border commercial communication is expanding and will expand further as new technology permits. In the Commission's view, there is already regulatory diversity, state by state, which is likely to impede market development. The Commission aims to keep developments under review, and suggests a system for pre-notifying it of new national initiatives.

29. COM (96) 192.

CHAPTER SEVEN

Product safety regulation

Community product safety policy

The development of a harmonized Community system of product safety regulation 'on paper' is far less problematic than harmonization in other sectors. It is hardly controversial to assert that there should be a requirement throughout the Community that unsafe products should not be placed on the market. To this extent, progress towards Community norms governing the health and safety of consumers raises far fewer fundamental questions of legal culture and regulatory technique than arise in the field of legal action to protect the economic interests of consumers. However, once one moves beyond a basic agreement that the law should forbid the marketing of unsafe goods, a number of problems impede the practical development of an effective Community product safety. How can the notion of 'safety' be given a common meaning? One may readily suppose that different approaches prevail in different parts of the Community. There are also fundamental questions about the enforcement strategies that are required to secure effective application of the Community rules. Community legislation establishes ground rules of safety; producers are putting in place integrated Community-wide marketing strategies; yet the patterns for enforcing the law are typically tied to national or even local level enforcement. How can information about dangerous goods and enforcement practice strategy be shared across borders? It will be seen that the Commission has secured a relatively limited power to act in its own right; that the Community has tried to establish systems of information sharing; but that also there have developed 'bottom-up' initiatives to elaborate a cross-border system. Nevertheless, there remains a gulf between the rapid evolution of an integrated product market in many sectors and the painfully slow progress towards integrated enforcement strategies. This is a significant problem in relation to product safety as such, but also in connection with the more general management of the internal market post-1992.[1]

The first measure to be discussed is Directive 88/378 on toy safety.[2] This is a harmonization measure designed to facilitate the growth of an integrated toy market on terms requiring a basic level of safety in products marketed. The structure of the Toy Safety Directive finds a close parallel in the more ambitious measure in the field adopted in 1992, Directive 92/59 on general product safety.[3] More generally, both Directives are fine illustrations of the Community's preferred regulatory technique in this area, the so-called 'new approach to technical harmonization'.[4] In the field of harmonization of technical rules, the new approach represents a shift in the legislative task from detailed rule-making in individual Directives to general policy articulation. The Community measure sets the broad target only, with reference to the 'essential safety requirements'. Elaboration is achieved through standards. Use of the new approach accelerates the legislative procedure, while loosening the grip on producers of over-rigid Community rules.

Toy safety – the structure of the Directive

The Toy Safety Directive takes Article 100a as its legal base. It provides a clear illustration of how a measure which is constitutionally rooted in internal market policy as a means of harmonizing national laws plays an inevitable role in developing a Community regulatory policy in the field which it occupies. In the Recitals to the Directive, it is explained that laws governing

---

1. H.-W. Micklitz (ed.), *Post Market Control of Consumer Goods* (Baden-Baden, Nomos, 1990);°H.-W. Micklitz, T. Roethe and S. Weatherill (eds), *Federalism and Responsibility: a study on Product Safety Law and Practice in the European Community* (London, Graham and Trotman, 1994); H.-W. Micklitz, *Internationales Produktsicherheitrecht* (Baden-Baden, Nomos, 1995).
2. OJ 1988 L187/1.   3. OJ 1992 L228/24.
4. Council Resolution of 7 May 1985 on a New Approach to technical harmonization and standards, OJ 1985 C136/1.

toy safety which differ between the member states cause barriers to trade. This is a rationale for the introduction of common rules. It is also explained that the content of the harmonized rule is related to the objectives of protecting consumer health and safety which were established by the Council in its resolution of June 1986, the third in the series of soft law resolutions which provide a framework for shaping Community consumer policy.[5] This serves as a clear expression of the dual focus of EC legislation which harmonizes laws concerning consumer protection. Formally, such legislation is a means to the end of market integration, yet, simultaneously, it exerts a significant influence on the development of Community consumer protection policy.

The common rules governing the safety of toys which are introduced by the Directive are found in Article 2, which provides that 'Toys may be placed on the market only if they do not jeopardize the safety and/or health of users or third parties when they are used as intended or in a foreseeable way'. The corollary is laid down in Article 4, which stipulates that 'Member states shall not impede the placing on the market on their territory of toys which satisfy the provisions of this Directive'. This reflects the pre-emptive consequence of the introduction of a common Community harmonized rule; this is no minimum measure.[6] Once traders comply with the required safety level, they are entitled to access to the market of all the member states. Consumers are thereby entitled to expect a wider choice of toys to become available, in accordance with the standard expectations of market integration. At the same time, the establishment and successful application of a basic safety level should serve to protect the consumer of toys from dangerous goods reaching the market.

Emphasis is typically placed on the rights of traders to gain access to markets by complying with the safety standards required by the Directive and the duty of states to accept such conforming goods on to their market. Nevertheless, it should not be neglected that the Directive also creates duties imposed on states to take action to forestall the marketing of unsafe goods. According to Article 3, 'Member states shall take all steps necessary to ensure that toys cannot be placed on the market unless they meet the essential safety requirements set out in

5. Chapter 1, p. 21.   6. Chapter 1, p. 14.

Annex II'. So there is a duty cast by Community law on the member states to secure safety standards. The protection of the consumer from unsafe goods is an aspect of the harmonization measure. This confirms the notion that Directives under Article 100a contribute to both market integration and market regulation.

The toy which complies with the essential safety requirements is entitled to free circulation. According to Article 7, a state which ascertains that toys bearing the 'CE' marking are not in conformity with the requirements of the Directive shall take action in respect of the product. The state must then inform the Commission of what it has done and why. This transmission of information permits the Commission to initiate procedures for consultation provided for in Article 7(2). It is critically important that management of action against unsafe items is envisaged in a *Community* context, not simply a national one. The development of state–Community channels of communication forms an essential component in the process of creating a comprehensive regulatory strategy designed to bring together national and Community authorities.

Toy safety – the new approach to technical harmonization

In line with the new approach to technical harmonization, the uniform Community rule refers to conformity with the 'essential safety requirements' and it is not the subject of exhaustive description in the Directive. Annex II to the Directive is entitled 'Essential Safety Requirements for Toys'. It provides an elaboration of what is intended by this notion. The emphasis of the Annex is on the overall objective to be achieved, not on specific methods whereby those objectives should be attained. This flexible style is aimed at providing incentives to manufacturers to pursue innovative techniques, to the ultimate benefit of the consumer. The finally adopted text of the Toy Safety Directive is in direct contrast to earlier drafts, which had followed a more detailed, technical style. Such proposals had not found favour with the Council.[7]

7. OJ 1980 C228/10; OJ 1983 C203/1.

According to Article 5(1) of the Directive, compliance with the essential requirements is to be presumed in respect of toys bearing the EC mark. In technical terms, the mark in practice consists of the symbol 'CE' according to Article 11(2). Moreover, the 'EC mark' is now properly referred to as the 'CE marking' as result of the amendments of Directive 93/68.[8] The CE marking denotes conformity with national standards which implement at national level harmonized European standards. Compliance with these standards permits an assumption of conformity to the Toy Safety Directive's essential requirements. The Recitals explain that the Community recognizes CEN and CENELEC as the competent bodies for the adoption of harmonized standards.

The CE marking is applied by the manufacturer, who ascertains that the toy conforms to the required standards and therefore to the essential safety requirements. The manufacturer must ensure that the product is suitable for the attachment of the mark and Article 8 of the Directive requires that relevant information be held. Supervision is then the responsibility of the member states[9] and Article 12 creates certain obligations in the sphere of inspection. However, it is fundamental to the pattern of regulation instituted by the Directive that the CE marking is *not* applied by the state. There is no system requiring prior approval of the toy. Doubtless, such a system would be regarded as disproportionately expensive in the toy sector, in contrast to some other areas, such as pharmaceuticals, where obligatory authorization prior to marketing plays a part in the system of supervision.

In conformity with the new approach's intention to lift inflexible regulatory burdens from traders, compliance with relevant standards is not mandatory from the point of view of the producer. There is another route for the producer to demonstrate conformity with the essential requirements. The producer can innovate by using a new design. Under Article 5(2) of the Directive, states shall presume that toys satisfy the essential safety requirements where, 'after receipt of an EEC type-examination certificate, their conformity with the approved model has been certified by the affixation of the [CE marking]'. The procedures for obtaining this type-examination certificate are found in Article 10. Approved bodies must be established by the member

8. OJ 1993 L220/1.   9. Art 3.

states for the purposes of type-examination in accordance with Article 9 and Annex III. The basic notion is that the approved body grants an EC type-examination certificate provided that the model complies with the essential safety requirements. There is, accordingly, made available an alternative route for producers to comply with the requirements of the Directive other than by simply adhering to existing standards.

The history of the Directive on general product safety

The Directive on general product safety generated political controversy. In the light of the pressures surrounding its negotiation, it underwent several revisions before it was finally adopted by the Council in 1992. In some respects it acts as a complement to Directive 85/374, the Product Liability Directive,[10] for it too concerns legal responses to unsafe products. However, whereas Directive 85/374 deals with the civil liability of the producer/supplier of an unsafe product and serves as no more than an indirect form of safety regulation by inducing the marketing of safe goods on pain of the imposition of private law liability owed to victims, Directive 92/59 operates as a more direct form of regulation of the market. Article 13 of Directive 92/59 asserts that the Directive applies without prejudice to Directive 85/374. It seeks to impose a general obligation on traders to prevent unsafe goods reaching the market in the first place.[11]

The Commission submitted a draft Directive in April 1989.[12] This was the subject of criticism on several levels and the Commission presented a further proposal in 1990.[13] Throughout, the legal basis remained Article 100a. As has already been commented in respect of the Toy Safety Directive, harmonization of safety laws integrates the market by establishing common standards throughout the territory of the Community on which

10. See Chapter 5.
11. G. Argiros, 'The EEC Directive on General Product Safety' [1994/1] LIEI 125 (1994); T. Askham and A. Stoneham, *EC Consumer Safety* (London, Butterworths, 1994).
12. OJ 1989 C193/1.
13. OJ 1990 C156/8.

traders may rely, but it also regulates that market by adopting a Community standard of required safety. Once again, this emphasizes the 'dual focus' of harmonization activity.

Directive 92/59 also follows the model of the Toy Safety Directive in the sense that it too is a classic new approach Directive. It does not seek to harmonize detailed laws relating to a particular product, but instead seeks to establish horizontal rules setting Community standards across a wide range of products. Those standards are drafted in a flexible manner, designed to permit and to encourage technological innovation.

Products covered

Article 2 of the Directive provides in paragraph (a) that, for the purposes of the Directive, 'product' means 'any product intended for consumers or likely to be used by consumers, supplied whether for consideration or not in the course of a commercial activity and whether new, used or reconditioned'.

According to paragraph (a) of Article 2, the Directive is inapplicable to second-hand products in two situations; where they are 'supplied as antiques or as products to be repaired or reconditioned prior to being used, provided that the supplier clearly informs the person to whom he supplies the product to that effect'. This limitation reflects concern on the part of some member states that the Directive might be drafted too broadly, and become an excessive regulatory burden. This is, in essence, a political value judgment; these exclusions reduce the scope of the measure as a means of consumer protection.

Persons covered

The terms 'producer' and 'distributor' are expanded in Articles 2(d) and (e), respectively. Obligations are imposed on such persons under Article 3. Article 3(1) provides that 'Producers shall be obliged to place only safe products on the market'. This is amplified in Article 3(2), which refers to obligations cast on producers to inform the consumer about risks inherent in the product where appropriate; and to enable themselves to be informed, as appropriate, about risks and to act accordingly, which may include product withdrawal. Accordingly, the producer bears a legal responsibility even after the product has been marketed. This is a commercially significant aspect of the regulatory regime instituted by the Directive.

By virtue of Article 3(3), distributors are drawn into this supervisory structure. They 'shall be required to act with due care in order to help to ensure compliance with the general safety requirement . . .'. This is a rather vague notion, which will depend for its practical content on implementation at national level. However, it is significant in that it expresses the network of obligations to ensure safety that is envisaged by the Directive.

Interrelation with existing rules

Fears of over-regulation of the market provided an impetus to make explicit provision for the relationship between the Directive and pre-existing Community rules of narrower substantive scope. Article 1(2) establishes a demarcation which precludes overlap between Directive 92/59 and other more specific measures. Where specific Community law rules contain provisions imposing safety requirements on the products which they govern, the basic provisions of Directive 92/59 shall *not* apply to those products. However, in the absence of such specific provisions governing safety, the general Directive shall apply. In fixing safety standards for products by Directive, there is to be neither overlap nor loophole.

The standard of safety

The standard which products must attain is set in accordance with the style of the new approach. There is no detailed set of specifications, which would stifle innovation. The objective is established by Article 1(1) of the Directive, which declares that 'The purpose of the provisions of this Directive is to ensure that products placed on the market are safe'.

Title II of the Directive, comprising Articles 3 and 4, is entitled 'General safety requirement'. Article 3(1) declares simply that 'Producers shall be obliged to place only safe products on the market'. Reference back to Article 2(b) amplifies the notion of 'safe product'. A safe product 'does not present any risk or only the minimum risks compatible with the product's use, considered as acceptable and consistent with a high level of protection for the safety and health of persons'.

Plainly, this is a flexible notion which will depend on the particular circumstances of a case. However, a list of points to be taken into account in making this assessment is supplied in Article 2(b) of the Directive. It includes, inter alia, the characteristics of the product, its presentation and the categories of consumers at serious risk when using the product (in particular, children). This assessment is stated to relate to 'normal or reasonably foreseeable conditions of use', which indicates that products must be safe even if *mis*used, if that misuse is reasonably foreseeable.[14] Product misuse – by children in particular – is notoriously common and, where reasonably foreseeable, it is therefore an element in safety assessment. So, for example, where a producer neglects to warn consumers that a product should not be used in a particular way that will cause harm, in circumstances where that misuse is foreseeable, it will be very difficult for a producer to claim successfully that the product is 'safe' simply by blaming the consumer for stepping beyond the bounds of normal usage. The message for producers is that possible harm should be anticipated and either forestalled through a modification of product design or, at least, brought clearly to the consumer's attention through instructions and/or warnings.

The standard of safety required under the Directive is plainly not absolute. A saw is designed to cut. If it causes an injury, it is not necessarily properly treated as unsafe. Some safe products carry an inevitable risk of causing injury. Naturally, in the case of risky products, traders are well-advised to pay special attention to the availability of devices that can reduce the risk, including appropriately bold warnings, since failure to take reasonable steps to minimize the risk will be relevant to the assessment of overall safety. Article 2(b) of the Directive provides that a product should present 'minimum risks compatible with . . . [its] use'. Provided this requirement has been met (and it will depend on the individual circumstances), the product is safe, notwithstanding that a person may have been injured by it.

---

14. This is readily comparable with the system of the Product Liability Directive (see Chapter 5).

A band of permissible safety is envisaged. The fact that one product may be *less safe* than another similar product does not automatically mean that the first product is *unsafe*. This is emphasized in the final paragraph of Article 2(b), which declares that 'The feasibility of obtaining higher levels of safety or the availability of other products presenting a lesser degree of risk shall not constitute grounds for considering a product to be unsafe or dangerous'. This is an important aspect of the chosen regulatory regime. Were the required standard of safety to be the highest attainable, then the apparent advantage to the consumer of high safety standards would be offset by the absence of choice and the raising of prices. Instead, the system establishes a safety requirement below the highest attainable level, allowing a market in products offering varying levels of protection from risk at (in a properly functioning market) prices which vary corresponding (inter alia) to the level of safety offered.

Under Article 4(1), a product is deemed safe when it conforms to the specific national law rules governing health and safety requirements of the state in whose territory the product is in circulation. This is a statement of the principle of mutual recognition, familiar from the European Court's *Cassis de Dijon* jurisprudence.[15] Under Article 4(2), the product's conformity to the general safety requirement is to be assessed –

> having regard to voluntary national standards giving effect to a European standard or, where they exist, to Community technical specifications or, failing these, to standards drawn up in the member state in which the product is in circulation, or to the codes of good practice in respect of health and safety in the sector concerned or to the state of the art and technology and to the safety which consumers may reasonably expect.

Article 4(3) establishes the competence which remains with the state into which the product is imported. Even where a product conforms to either Article 4(1) or 4(2), national authorities are able to restrict its access to the market or to secure its withdrawal from the market 'where there is evidence that, despite such conformity, it is dangerous to the health and safety of consumers'. It will be explained below that such action must be managed within a Community framework.

[15.] Chapter 2, p. 44.

Enforcement by member states

Implementation of the Directive by the member states involves, inter alia, securing the enforcement of the pattern of obligations imposed on producers and distributors to market only safe products. One approach would have been simply to exclude from the Directive any reference to national methods of enforcement and to rely on the member states to shape enforcement structures in line with national tradition. This would place on national authorities the general obligation of effective implementation, rooted in Articles 5 and 189 of the Treaty. However, the Directive as finally adopted is rather more ambitious. It makes limited progress towards the specification of the institutional support and enforcement techniques that are required as a matter of Community law. This issue caused much of the controversy in the several draft proposals which were rejected prior to the final successful adoption of the Directive in 1992.

Title III, comprising Articles 5 and 6, contains the 'Obligations and powers of the member states'. Article 5 declares that 'Member states shall adopt the necessary laws, regulations and administrative provisions to make producers and distributors comply with their obligations under this Directive in such a way that products placed on the market are safe'.

In itself, this is little more than an application of the general Article 5/189 EC obligation to the specific area covered by this Directive. Article 5 of the Directive proceeds to offer amplification in requiring member states to establish or nominate authorities empowered to monitor the application of the law and to take the measures required under the Directive, which shall include the possibility of imposing penalties in the event of infringement. Article 6 stipulates that member states shall have the necessary powers to adopt appropriate measures to achieve a list of objectives, including, for example, safety checks, publication of warnings, product bans and product withdrawal.

Article 7 places action taken in the context of an integrating market. Where states restrain the marketing of a product, they shall inform the Commission, excepting only situations without cross-border implications. Article 7(2) directs the Commission to consult on the matter and then to inform all the member states where it considers the measure justified or to inform the notifying state alone where it considers the measure unjustified. Article 7 thus envisages a system for sharing information which draws together Community and national authorities. It is significant in opening a route to integrated cross-border enforcement strategies, needed in the wake of the accelerating product market integration, which makes it increasingly improbable that problems of unsafe goods will have purely local impacts.

The powers of the Commission

The Directive also confers powers on the Commission. Title V, which comprises Articles 8–12 deals with 'Emergency situations and action at Community level'. Whereas Articles 5 and 6 of the Directive, examined above, assume action taken at national level and attempt to locate that action within a managed Community framework, Title V of the Directive confers powers on the Commission to act in the sphere of product safety. This is one of the most controversial aspects of the Directive.[16]

Articles 9–11 govern the powers of the Commission to act. They arise where there exists 'a serious and immediate risk from a product to the health and safety of consumers in various member states'. That condition is necessary but not sufficient. Article 9 also includes a list of four further hurdles, (a)–(d), all of which must be crossed. These hurdles concern a requirement of prior action taken against the product by at least one member state; divergence between member states on the adoption of measures; inability to deal with the risk under other procedures; and the requirement that the risk can be eliminated effectively only by the adoption of appropriate measures applicable at Community level. These hurdles satisfied, the Commission must then consult the member states and must receive a request from at least one of them. It may then adopt a decision requiring member states to take temporary measures drawn from those listed in Articles 6(1)(d)–(h).

The decision is to be adopted in accordance with the procedure set out in Article 11. This requires the Commission to submit proposed measures to a Committee on Product Safety Emergencies, composed, in accordance with Article 10, of the

16. See generally, C. Joerges, 'Social Regulation and the Legal Structure of the EEC' in B. Stauder (ed.), *La Sécurité des produits de consommation* (Zürich, Schulthess, 1992).

representatives of the member states. Article 11(1) contains the detailed rules governing the delivery of the Committee's opinion and the consequences thereof. Article 11(2) provides that any measure adopted shall be valid for no more than three months. Under Article 11(3), member states shall implement decisions within less than ten days.

This procedure is important as a step beyond the notion that the Commission performs no more than a function of information transmission and general supervision of implementation by the member states. Articles 9–11 of the Directive place a power of administrative decision making in the hands of the Commission. This allocation of power contains the seeds of a Europeanization of product safety policy. However, such ambitious theoretical notions must be tempered by practical reality. Articles 9–11 are subject to significant threshold criteria. One may even go so far as to suppose that the pre-conditions to Commission action will virtually never be satisfied. Certainly, Articles 9–11, as adopted, confer a power to act which falls far short of more ambitious calls in the past for a Europeanized control system. It is, for example, remote from the notion of a Community product recall procedure suggested by the Consumers Consultative Committee.[17] Earlier drafts of the Directive had contained less stringent criteria which had to be met before the Commission could act. The Commission's 1989 draft required neither prior action to have been taken against the product by at least one member state, nor divergence between member states on the adoption of measures.[18] That would probably still have given rise to very few instances where the Commission would have been able to act, yet the member states still preferred to insert extra pre-conditions before final adoption of the Directive.

Directive 92/59 before the European Court

Acute political sensitivity surrounds the question of equipping the Commission with administrative powers in the field. Even the

17. CCC/107/79, CCC/66/82.
18. OJ 1989 C193/1; D. Hoffmann, 'Product safety in the internal market: the proposed Community emergency procedure' in M. Fallon and F. Maniet (eds), *Product safety and control processes in the European Community* (Brussels, Story Scientia/CDC, 1990).

relatively narrow competence to act conferred on the Commission by Article 9 of the Directive provoked a challenge to the validity of the measure by Germany. *Germany v Council*[19] involved an application under Article 173 for annulment of Article 9 of the Directive. The action was unsuccessful and the Court's ruling is important in its acceptance that Article 100a EC has a valid role to play beyond simple harmonization of laws 'on paper'. Nevertheless, the fact that Germany, unable to exercise a political veto because Article 100a requires only a QMV in Council in favour of a proposal, felt it necessary to pursue the matter to the European Court is evidence of current political concerns about the scope of Community legislative competence.

Germany did not express an objection to the harmonization of safety standards. Instead, it challenged Article 9 of the Directive in so far as it empowered the Commission to adopt decisions requiring the member states to take named measures in respect of products. Germany submitted that Article 9 lacked a legal base and that it violated the principle of proportionality. Germany claimed that all that could be drawn from Article 100a was a power conferred on the Commission to check whether provisional national measures comply with Community law and not to adopt measures itself. This view is transparently driven by a narrow interpretation of the scope of Article 100a as a means of building Community power and a corresponding emphasis on the primary role of implementation at national level as a means of realizing Community objectives expressed in Directives. Were such an approach to prevail, the potential for Europeanization of enforcement structures would be severely circumscribed, at least via Article 100a. Germany's concern to fix the boundaries between Community and national competence was further reflected in its observation that Article 9 of Directive 92/59 conferred more power to the Commission than would be allowed the *Bund* at the expense of the *Länder* in the context of German federalism.

The Court rejected the German application, concluding that action at Community level of the type envisaged by Article 9 was justified in order to protect the health and safety of consumers and to ensure the proper functioning of the market. The Court considered that Article 100a empowered the Council to take

19. Case C-359/92 [1994] ECR I-3681.

measures aimed at the establishment and functioning of the internal market. In some sectors, particularly that of product safety, harmonization of laws alone may not be adequate to achieve this objective. The Court accepted that measures within the meaning of Article 100a 'must be interpreted as encompassing the Council's power to lay down measures relating to a specific product or class of products and, if necessary, individual measures concerning those products'.[20] The Court was, unsurprisingly, unreceptive to the German suggestion that the relationship between Community and member state powers should be analysed with reference to national constitutional patterns. It simply observed that the relationship between Community and its member states is not the same as that between *Bund* and *Länder*. The Court was also unpersuaded by the rather flimsy submission that Article 9 contravened the principle of proportionality. It stated that the powers conferred were appropriate to achieve the objectives pursued and did not go beyond what was necessary in relation to those objectives.

The issue underlying this litigation is political resistance in some quarters to the capacity of the Community to construct Europeanized institutional structures in support of the process of market integration. The Court's ruling provides no general method for resolving such tensions; nor could the Court be expected to resolve such fundamental political questions about the development of federalism in Europe. Within the sector of product safety, at least, the Court's ruling in this case upholds the validity of the use of Article 100a EC in order to move beyond a pattern of harmonization of laws which relies exclusively on national systems for implementation.

Information sharing – RAPEX

The significance of administrative coordination as a means of achieving both market integration and effective consumer protection in the Community should not be underestimated. There are two distinct aspects to the role of administrative coordination. First, it acts as a complement to substantive rules and ensures that they may achieve their objective. Common

---

20. Para. 37 of the judgment.

Community rule making must be accompanied by a pattern of common strategies for the application and enforcement of those rules. This is a matter which has gained an increasingly high profile since the completion of the internal market. Secondly, the development of administrative coordination is itself part of the process of developing a Community consumer law and policy, even where it occurs independently of the existence of specific Community initiatives.

This should be linked, at a much more general level, with the prescriptions contained in the Sutherland Report, published in October 1992.[21] This emphasized that the operation of the internal market depends for its success on much greater cooperation between national and Community institutions. It envisaged a growth of administrative partnership to enhance the practical application of the rules. This has served subsequently as a basis for Commission thinking.[22]

The Community first put in place a system for the rapid exchange of information on dangers arising from the use of consumer products in 1984.[23] The system, commonly abbreviated from 'Rapid Exchange' to 'RAPEX', provides for the transmission of information about urgent measures taken at national level because of 'the serious and immediate risk which that product or product batch presents for the health or safety of consumers when used in normal and foreseeable conditions'. The state must inform the Commission, which then forwards information to other member states. Those states then alert the Commission to any measures they have taken, which is then communicated to the other states. Detailed agreed procedures govern the practical operation of the scheme. Plainly, the system reflects the need for a cross-border dimension to effective enforcement policy in the sphere of product safety, in the light of the cross-border commercial strategies undertaken by traders in an integrated market.

The system was initially set up in 1984 for a four-year trial period. In 1988 the Commission proposed that that period be

---

21. The Internal Market after 1992: Meeting the Challenge, Report to the EEC Commission by the High Level Group on the Operation of Internal Market.
22. For example, Commission Communication on the development of administrative cooperation in the implementation and enforcement of Community legislation in the Internal Market, COM (94) 29.
23. Council Decision 84/133 EEC, OJ 1984 L70/16.

extended to ten years.[24] It prepared a report on the operation of the system which was broadly favourable, although it admitted that use of the notification procedure had been rather erratic.[25] However, in December 1988 the Council decided that it would renew the system only until 30 June 1990.[26] The debate about RAPEX was conducted in the shadow of discussion of the proposed Directive on general product safety, which would be adopted only in 1992, for it was envisaged that the legal provisions governing RAPEX would be brought within that Directive, once adopted, as part of the construction of a comprehensive Community system dealing with product safety. In 1990 it was therefore agreed in Council that the system would once again be renewed, on this occasion until the date for implementing the Directive on general product safety.[27] In 1992, when the Directive was finally adopted, RAPEX was accommodated within it in Article 8, amplified by an Annex to the Directive. Decision 89/45 was repealed on 29 June 1994 by Article 18 of Directive 92/59.

Article 8 of the Directive is essentially concerned to place the Rapid Exchange system on a formal footing within the Directive. Article 8(1) imposes notification requirements on states which take 'emergency' measures against products posing 'a serious and immediate risk' to the health and safety of consumers. Article 8(2) requires the Commission, on receipt of the information, to check its compliance with the terms of the Directive, and then to forward it to other member states. Other states shall then inform the Commission of any measures adopted. This system envisages the sharing of information in order to reduce the inefficiencies brought about where the same problem is tackled by different authorities in different states taking different approaches with different levels of available information. However, Article 8 establishes the Commission as the channel through which information is routed, not as a filter of that information, nor even as an initiator. The assumption remains that the initial decision whether to intervene in the market rests with the member state(s), albeit acting within a framework governed by substantive Community rules on product safety.

---

24. OJ 1988 C124/9.   25. OJ 1988 C146/8.
26. Council Decision 89/45 EEC, OJ 1989 L17/51.
27. Council Decision 90/352 EEC, OJ 1990 L173/49.

Article 8(3) states that detailed procedures are to be found in an Annex to the Directive, which aims to set out stage-by-stage management of a product safety emergency, combining information sharing and action at both national and Community level. Paragraph 2 of the Annex concedes that immediate and serious risks cannot be defined with precision in advance and that national authorities must therefore judge cases on their merits. One may readily speculate that the proviso of 'serious and immediate' risk will be interpreted in different ways in different states. Indeed, this is conceded by the Commission. A 1993 Commission report on the handling of urgent situations in the context of implementation of Community rules admits to a rather erratic pattern of notification under the System.[28] The Commission declares an intention to establish guidelines (which have now been drawn up) with a view to achieving a more common approach to notification. The report also reveals that the follow-up to notifications is patchy. Of all notifications relating to non-food products, only seven out of the then twelve member states on average replied to notifications; 89 days was the average time for reply.

Ideally, RAPEX would buttress the substantive rules in the field of product safety, which provide the basis for determining whether goods may be marketed, by instituting structures for cross-border sharing of information which would form the foundation for effective application and enforcement of such rules throughout the Community. In practice, its impact is erratic. It is only a starting point in building effective cooperation between responsible national and Community authorities in the discharge of their obligations in the field of product safety.

Beyond RAPEX

Some progress beyond RAPEX has been made at Community level. A Community system for the exchange of information in respect of certain products which may jeopardize consumers' health and safety was instituted as a result of a Council decision of 1993.[29] This complements RAPEX by providing for information transmission about hazardous goods which do not present

[28] COM (93) 430. [29] Decision 93/580/EEC, OJ 1993 L278/64.

the 'serious and immediate risk', which is the threshold for transfer of information under RAPEX.

However, it is important to appreciate that while the improvement of administrative cooperation in pursuit of more effective supervision of the integrating market is of fundamental importance, this objective cannot be achieved simply by 'top-down' Community legislative instruments. Cooperation has developed across borders spontaneously, as enforcement agencies find that they cannot properly perform their functions in an integrating market without establishing connections with counterparts in other states.[30] Such 'bottom-up' initiatives may be patchy in their geographical coverage; they may by-pass the Commission and even central government within individual member states. Partly as a consequence of the essentially informal nature of these linkages between administrative agencies in different states, an exhaustive, empirically observed description of the patterns of links which have been established cannot feasibly be supplied. Developments are dynamic, not static. However, they represent a significant development in practical product safety law and policy. Indeed, it should not be overlooked that such initiatives, driven by local knowledge and an awareness of practical problem-solving, may produce a better *informed* system than can be devised at the more abstract level of legislative planning, remote from practical enforcement. In so far as agencies in different states are induced to co-operate in overcoming the obstacle of administrative heterogeneity between the member states, the 'bottom-up' system reflects desirable features of the notion of subsidiarity. The paper on subsidiarity annexed to the Conclusions of the Presidency which emerged from the 1992 Edinburgh European Council[31] commented that:

> Where appropriate under the Treaty, and provided this is sufficient to achieve its objectives, preference in choosing the type of Community action should be given to encouraging cooperation between member states, coordinating national action or to complementing, supplementing or supporting such action.

---

[30] S. Weatherill, 'The Reinvigoration of Community Product Safety Policy' 14 Journal of Consumer Policy 171 (1991); S. Weatherill, 'Playing Safe: the UK's Implementation of the Toy Safety Directive' in T. Daintith (ed.), *Implementing EC Law in the UK* (Chichester, Wiley Chancery, 1995), ch. 9.

[31] Chapter 1, p. 33.

The Commission has adopted this perspective in the area of product safety enforcement and has provided funding for some initiatives that began at grass-roots enforcement level, without explicit legislative support at either Community or national level. In the UK, the Local Authorities Co-ordinating Body on Trading Standards, a non-statutory body set up by local government (LACOTS), pursued inquiries into the identity of counterparts in other member states, a task which is plainly vital as a starting point in developing an enforcement strategy involving a cross-border dimension. It produced the fruits of such research in two booklets produced in 1992; *Consumer Product Safety* and *Consumer Protection Control Bodies*. The first named booklet provides a list of the addresses of agencies with responsibility for enforcing consumer product safety laws in each of the (then) twelve member states. The second booklet is similarly structured, but is broader in its coverage, extending beyond matters of safety alone. These booklets provide valuable basic information and reflect the developing practice of administrative cooperation. The Commission part-funded LACOTS in its work in this field. This is but one example of an important aspect of practical enforcement policy.

CHAPTER EIGHT

Access to justice

The implementation of Directives

Although harmonization Directives ought to act as a source of consumer protection at national level, it is necessary to assess the effectiveness of the system for securing vindication of those legal rules. There are at least two separate elements to this inquiry. The first relates to the constitutional question of the extent to which Directives can create 'rights' on which individuals may rely. The second, discussed later in this chapter, relates to more practical questions of the extent to which consumer protection law on paper offers a framework for improving the consumer's lot in everyday life. In the EC context, this second, practical matter raises particular questions about the ability of a cross-border consumer to assert legal rights against a trader located in a state other than his or her own.

The text of Article 189 EC appears to exclude the possibility that Directives can create rights that are enforceable directly by individuals. Article 189 stipulates that a Directive is 'binding, as to the result to be achieved, upon each member state to which it is addressed, but shall leave to the national authorities the choice of form and methods'. Directives appear incapable of direct effect, for their impact is conditional on national implementing measures. In unimplemented guise they seem inapt for judicial enforcement.

The obligation created by EC law rests with the state, which must secure implementation of the requirements of the Directive within the national legal order in conformity with the obligation found in Article 5 EC. The precise details of the implementation process remain to be elaborated at national level. This is the strength of the Directive as a legal instrument, in that it allows norms derived from Community law to be absorbed into established national structures; yet it is simultaneously a weakness, in that the Community law origins of the legal rule may be obscured, and their impact diluted, by its indirect route into the national legal order.[1]

The field of consumer law provides examples of Directives which go beyond the normal assumption that it is for the national authorities to select methods of effective implementation which suit their traditions. Directive 93/13 on unfair terms in consumer contracts and Directive 84/450 on misleading advertising both include more specific provisions that envisage enforcement by public agencies.[2] The Commission appears to find this system attractive and is contemplating proposing its addition to the regime on consumer credit.[3] Although these provisions do not explicitly require as a matter of Community law that consumer representative organizations be granted special powers to initiate proceedings, it is an intriguing argument that equipping consumer organizations with such powers is required as part of the Treaty obligation to establish adequate and effective control mechanisms.[4]

Where a member state fails to comply with the obligation drawn from Articles 5 and 189 EC effectively to implement a Directive at national level, the principal remedy explicitly envisaged in the Treaty involves Commission investigation, which may ultimately lead to a ruling of the European Court that the state has failed to comply with its Treaty obligations. This is the Article 169 procedure. It is open to anyone to complain to the Commission that EC law is being flouted and to request the Commission to act. However, the Commission's resources are scarce and it deploys them according to its administrative priorities. Although specific legislative provision, elaborated through case law, confers special protection for the consumer complainant in the area of competition policy,[5] there is no

---

[1.] T. Daintith (ed.), *Implementing EC Law in the UK: Structures for Indirect Rule* (Chichester, John Wiley, 1995).

[2.] Chapters 4 and 6.   [3.] Chapter 3: COM (95) 117, para. 27.

[4.] Questions of this nature have been referred to the European Court (Case C-82/96) in connection with the UK's implementation of Directive 93/13, which denies consumer bodies any special standing.

[5.] Art. 3(2)(b), Reg. 17/62; cf. Case T-37/92 *B.E.U.C. v Commission* [1994] ECR II-285.

general possibility for the consumer to insist that the Commission shall investigate an alleged state failure to comply with Community consumer policy. The Court has made it clear that the Commission's discretion to initiate Article 169 proceedings may not be the subject of judicial review initiated by an individual.[6] It seems that a consumer representative organization would be equally powerless. This leaves only the option of pursuing the alleged infraction of Community law through proceedings initiated at national level.

But nothing in the explicit terms of the Treaty suggests that an individual derives any right directly from a Directive, nor that an individual can challenge a state's failure to implement. This leaves the consumer, like the employee and other interested beneficiaries of legal protection envisaged under a Directive, dependent on faithful implementation by the member state. Faulty implementation of Directives is a regrettably common phenomenon. In consequence, rights that ought to be enjoyed by individuals remain contingent on the member state being driven to comply with Treaty obligations.

The impact of Directives within the national legal order

It is well known that the European Court has developed the constitutional impact of Community law within the national legal order beyond that envisaged by the explicit terms of the Treaty.[7] In certain circumstances, an unimplemented Directive may generate legal effects within the national system which benefit the individual, including the consumer. Notwithstanding the apparent blockage caused by the need for state implementation, which stands between the Community legislature and the private individual in the case of a Directive, the European Court has refused to allow a state's failure to implement to subvert entirely the intended conferral of rights on an individual.[8] In this vein, the

---

6. Case 247/87 *Star Fruit v Commission* [1989] ECR 291.
7. S. Weatherill and P. Beaumont, *EC Law* (London, Penguin Books, 2nd edn, 1995); T. Hartley, *The Foundations of EC Law* (Oxford, Clarendon Press, 3rd edn, 1994).
8. S. Prechal, *Directives in EC Law* (Oxford, OUP, 1995).

European Court in *Ratti*[9] held that Directives are capable of invocation before national courts. An individual acting in conformity with a Directive left unimplemented after its deadline by Italy was able to rely on the Directive to defeat a prosecution under an Italian law that should already have been repealed.

However, the Court is not prepared to allow a private individual to rely on an unimplemented Directive other than in proceedings where the other party is the state. This is *vertical* direct effect, of which Directives are capable; but Directives are not *horizontally* directly effective, that is, they may not be invoked directly in relations between private parties before national courts. The Court's refusal to countenance the horizontal direct effect of Directives was established in *Marshall v Southampton Area Health Authority*,[10] a case arising in the sphere of sex discrimination. The principal objection to attributing horizontal direct effect to an unimplemented Directive was the Court's perception that it is the state, not a private individual, which is at fault, and that it would accordingly be improper to interpret the constitutional reach of the unimplemented Directive in such a way as to impose obligations on an 'innocent' private party. This is a significant problem for the consumer. The consumer wishing to rely on an unimplemented Directive will succeed where the supplier is the 'state', which for these purposes is broadly interpreted to include local authorities[11] and even private entities which possess 'special powers beyond those which result from the normal rules applicable in relations between individuals'.[12] However, beyond the reach of the public sector, even broadly defined, Directives are incapable of direct effect. Typically, the protection envisaged by an EC Directive in the consumer field will relate to private relationships between consumer and supplier. Accordingly, the consumer will remain dependent on faithful national implementation for legal protection.

The Court made a separate advance in its campaign to attribute an impact at national level to unimplemented Directives by insisting that national courts fall under an obligation, drawn from Article 5, 'to interpret national law ... in every way

---

[9] Case 148/78 [1979] ECR 1629. [10] Case 152/84 [1986] ECR 723.
[11] Case 103/88 *Fratelli Costazo v Milano* [1989] ECR 1839.
[12] Case C-188/89 *Foster v British Gas* [1990] ECR I-3133.

possible ... to achieve the results envisaged by [a Directive]'. This notion, that national courts shall secure the 'indirect effect' of a Directive, applies to 'national law, whether the provisions concerned pre-date or post-date the Directive'.[13] Through this technique, an unimplemented Directive could penetrate the national legal order. However, the Court's use of Article 5 in this fashion has been criticized on several counts. It has been suggested that, by asking national courts to repair the deficiencies of the legislature, it violates the principle of separation of powers. At a more practical level, it is unclear whether the variety of approaches to the obligation of interpretation which will doubtless be taken by different courts in different states serves to instil adequate reliability and uniformity in the (indirect) application of Community law. A perhaps constitutionally more appropriate, and potentially practically more effective, route is to focus on the liability of the member state which has failed to implement a Directive to compensate private individuals who have suffered loss in consequence on the default. The European Court added this means of individual legal protection in *Francovich v Italian State*,[14] a case which arose in the sphere of employment protection but which expressed a principle of wider application. The Court declared that:

> The full effectiveness of Community rules would be impaired and the protection of the rights which they grant would be weakened if individuals were unable to obtain redress when their rights are infringed by a breach of Community law for which a member state can be held responsible.

It identified three elements of liability:

> The first of those conditions is that the result prescribed by the directive should entail the grant of rights to individuals. The second condition is that it should be possible to identify the content of those rights on the basis of the provisions of the directive. Finally, the third condition is the existence of a causal link between the breach of the state's obligation and the loss and damage suffered by the injured parties.

---

13. Case C-106/89 *Marleasing v La Comercial Internacional de Alimentacion* [1990] ECR I-4135.
14. Cases C-6, C-9/90 [1991] ECR I-5357.

Having established these three conditions, the Court ͺ
that the state must make reparation for the consequenͼ
damage caused 'on the basis of the rules of national
liability' and that 'it is for the internal legal order oɪ
member state to designate the competent courts and lay dowɪ. ͽ
detailed procedural rules'.

This shifts the focus of the individual's claim away from the
identity of the party (private or public) against which rights under
the Directive are envisaged towards the state as the party
responsible under the EC Treaty for putting rights in place in the
national legal order. In this sense, a *Francovich* claim is a more
direct method of protection for the individual prejudiced by
non-implementation of a Directive, although claims based on the
direct and indirect effect of Directives are also still available. The
Court has moved a considerable distance beyond the explicit
terms of the Treaty in its quest to secure effective protection of
Community law rights at national level.[15]

Denial of horizontal direct effect

But one element still remains absent from this pattern of legal
protection: horizontal direct effect. An unimplemented Directive
is not capable of generating rights which one private individual is
able to enforce against another private individual. The Court's
refusal to countenance *horizontal* direct effect of Directives has
been subjected to criticism, inter alia, on the basis that it
undermined effective legal protection and that it led to inequality
of citizens before the law, since the impact of Directives varied
across the territory of the Union depending on the patterns of
implementation state by state. Yet the Court, even when faced
with strong assertions by Advocates-General that the horizontal
direct effect of Directives should be embraced,[16] chose to

15. D. Curtin and K. Mortelmans, 'Application and Enforcement of Community
Law by the Member States: Actors in Search of a Third Generation Script' in
D. Curtin and T. Heukels (eds), *Institutional Dynamics of European
Integration* (Dordrecht, Martinus Nijhoff, 1994).
16. A-G Van Gerven in Case C-271/91 *Marshall (2)* [1993] 3 CMLR 293, A-G
Jacobs in Case C-316/93 *Vaneetveld v SA Le Foyer* [1994] ECR I-763, A-G
Lenz in *Dori* itself.

re-affirm its refusal to adopt that course in *Faccini Paola Dori v Recreb Srl.*[17] This ruling was delivered in the context of the non-implementation of a Directive in the consumer field. It is therefore richly illustrative of the obstacles to consumer access to justice which flow from the Court's stance.

Italy had failed to implement Directive 85/577 on doorstep selling.[18] On Milan Railway Station, Ms Dori was lured into a contract covered by the Directive by a seller of educational material. Under the Directive, she should have been entitled to claim a right to withdraw from the deal and, having 'cooled off', she decided that she wished to exercise that right. Under Italian law no such right existed. She was thus bound to the deal unless she was able to plead the Directive before the Italian courts against the supplier, a private party. In an Article 177 ruling, the European Court adhered to *Marshall* and held that the Directive could not be directly effective in such circumstances. Plainly, Ms Dori was denied a right which she was supposed to enjoy under a Directive. A loophole in the practical vigour of EC consumer protection law was exposed.

In refusing to accept that the consumer could rely on the terms of the Directive to defend an action brought before a national court by the supplier, the Court mentioned the availability to Ms Dori of an action against the state based on *Francovich*. This may be welcome in theory, but in practice it seems unrealistic. The daunting prospect of pursuing an action against the state to recover a relatively small sum would dissuade the vast majority of consumers. The Court also mentioned the obligation of the national court to interpret national law in the light of the Directive, but the fragilities of this route have already been mentioned above; it is rather uncertain, dependent on national judicial capability and willingness. A consumer in such circumstances simply wishes to exercise a right to withdraw from a contract, involving, if necessary, a suitable defence to a claim for breach of contract where he or she refuses to pay sums due. This is the effective method of protecting consumer rights and it is the effective method of securing observance of Directives evenly throughout the territory of the Community. Yet the Court in *Dori* asserted that the Community is not competent to enact by Directive obligations for individuals with immediate effects. The

17. Case C-91/92 [1994] ECR I-3325.   18. Chapter 3.

Court confirmed that it is unreceptive to submissions that Directives should be regarded as capable of horizontal direct effect in *El Corte Inglés SA v Cristina Blázquez Rivero*,[19] where a consumer was held unable to rely on Directive 87/102 on consumer credit,[20] which had not been implemented in Spain, in proceedings brought against her by a private lender. The Court decided that the insertion of Article 129a on consumer protection into the EC Treaty at Maastricht made no difference to its refusal to attribute horizontal direct effect to Directives.

The denial of horizontal direct effect robs the Directive of some of its vitality as a method of creating consumer rights within the national system. It is especially damaging to the typical 'small-scale' consumer claimant in litigation with a trader, whether as plaintiff or as defendant. It also wrecks the even application of consumer law state by state. A consumer who shops in a member state other than his or her own will *not* be confident that Community law has set effective minimum standards of protection. If that state has not properly implemented the Directive, the consumer will have no directly enforceable right against a private supplier. The absence of horizontal direct effect contradicts the policy found in, for example, the recitals to the Directive on unfair terms in consumer contracts[21] that consumer confidence in cross-border shopping should be engendered by the creation of Community-wide minimum standards. Where the state has failed to meet its obligation to implement, the right to 'cool off', for example, will be unavailable; so, too, the right to evade the enforceability of unfair terms. The consumer will be left with only the costly direct action against the state envisaged by *Francovich* and the unpredictable route of seeking to persuade the national judge to interpret existing national law in the light of the Directive, as required by Article 5 EC.

Practical access to justice

Even assuming that Directives are faithfully implemented at national level and their application adequately policed, there

---

[19]. Case C-192/94 judgment of 7 March 1996.
[20]. Chapter 3.   [21]. Chapter 4.

remain fundamental questions about the extent to which the consumer is able to derive practical advantage from them. There are doubts as to whether consumers even *know* of the extent of their legal rights. There are doubts whether they are able to use them in practice to persuade a reluctant trader to resolve a dispute. Literally the last thing a consumer wants to do is to go to the expense and delay of pursuing formal proceedings in court. Consumers frequently simply write off disappointing purchases. These are problems in any national system, where consumer law on paper means little in practice if it is unknown or unused. The problems are magnified where the consumer meets a problem in another member state, where, for all the progress made in legal harmonization, procedures are likely to be intimidatingly unfamiliar.[22]

The first Council Resolution on a preliminary programme for a consumer protection and information policy, adopted in 1975,[23] included in its list of five basic rights both the right of redress and the right to information and education. However, the development of these rights and aims through specific measures at Community level has been minimal. The development of EC consumer law on paper has not been matched by concrete steps towards improvement of access to justice in the cross-border context.[24]

Education has typically been regarded as essentially a national matter. Even the new Article 129a EC suggests a subordinate role for EC initiatives. EC action will supplement 'the policy pursued by the member states to protect the health, safety and economic interests of consumers and to provide adequate information to consumers'. Consumer redress remains largely a national matter.

In June 1987, the Council adopted a Resolution on consumer redress which referred to the problems faced by aggrieved consumers in the integrating market.[25] It was broadly favourable to the idea of further work in the field as preparation for a possible Community initiative, although the Council remained non-committal on specific action. The Commission's subsequent investigation left it acutely aware of the difficulties that a consumer faced in securing access to justice in a state other than

---

22. K. Viitanen, 'Consumer Redress' Consum LJ 6 (1995).
23. Chapter 1, p. 9.
24. M. Goyens, 'EC Policy with regard to Consumer Redress' Consum LJ 35 (1995).
25. OJ 1987 C176/2.

his or her own. It believed that this disincentive to shop across borders jeopardized the process of constructing the internal market. The 1992 Sutherland Report placed similar emphasis on the active, cross-border consumer as a potential instrument for breaking down national barriers.[26] However, the Commission also remained aware that its role lay primarily in the area of encouraging new initiatives. One cannot feasibly legislate 'effective access to justice' into being.

The 1993 Green Paper

The Commission published a Green Paper on Access to Justice in November 1993.[27] It starts from the premise that access to justice is uniquely problematic in the EC because of the different procedures which apply in the legal systems of different member states. There is no 'European legal space'. As cross-border consumer activity has grown increasingly realistic since the completion of the internal market, so the problems associated with subjecting the resolution of disputes to purely national procedures have become ever more severe. A consumer wishing to pursue a complaint in a jurisdiction other than his or her own will be confronted by unfamiliar rules, which may deter pursuit of the grievance, and which in turn may deter taking advantage of the internal market in the first place.

The Green Paper follows the Sutherland Report in assuming that the current pattern of private international law falls far short of an adequate solution. Relevant Conventions are of relatively limited scope, and, in particular, as a consequence of their focus on passive consumers who do not leave their own state, they do little for the active, cross-border consumer, whom the Commission wishes to encourage. In any event, none of the Conventions is in force in all the member states.[28]

The Green Paper notes that it is common in the Community for administrative bodies and/or consumer organizations to have standing to take legal proceedings to suppress unlawful

26. The Internal Market after 1992: Meeting the Challenge: Report to the EEC Commission by the High Level Group on the Operation of the Internal Market.
27. COM (93) 576.
28. J. Y. Carlier, *Guide des litiges transfrontalières* (Paris, Institut National de la Consommation, 1995).

commercial practices. Such collective action represents an important mechanism for securing law enforcement in the light of the inability of an individual consumer relying on the private law effectively to dissuade widespread malpractice. However, such collective action tends to break down where transfrontier issues arise. Agencies in the state where loss is suffered typically lack capacity to take legal action because they are not the national bodies of the offending country; agencies in the state whence the practice originated typically lack an interest in pursuing the matter, since 'their' consumers are not affected. The Green Paper adopts as a theme for discussion the possibility of creating a system which would allow the free movement of actions for an injunction.

The Green Paper also discusses the possible institution of a follow-up mechanism for transfrontier complaints. This would be designed to identify the problems encountered and to establish priorities for their resolution. This could involve the promotion of codes of conduct for self-regulatory schemes, including those based on an ombud system. The construction of cooperative systems across borders involving administrative and enforcement agencies and consumer representative organisations could be an element. Such notions reflect the evolving educational process which the Commission aims to set in train. Only once it has identified the nature of the problems can it begin to shape more ambitious proposals at Community level for their resolution.

Since the 1993 Green Paper

The Commission remains concerned to develop concrete ideas in order to convey information to consumers about how to take advantage of the completion of the internal market. For example, in 1994 the Commission published the *European consumer guide to the single market*. According to the foreword, written by Christiane Scrivener, then Commissioner responsible for consumer policy, the guide was designed to 'set out the plain facts on the European dimension of consumer protection. We want to give our readers the confidence necessary to explore the advantages of the single market and play a part in building it.' A second edition was published in 1996; the responsible Commissioner, Emma Bonino, displayed continuity by penning more or less the same foreword. The guide is written in plain language rather than legal jargon.[29] The Commission also helped to establish European Consumer Information Centres ('Euroguichets'), which act as advice centres for consumers in trans-frontier regions. Ten of these pilot projects were established by the start of 1993 and by the start of 1996 there were 21 (including 'outstations' of main centres). The Commission aims to cooperate with national authorities in facilitating the pursuit of consumer complaints.

Moreover, as has already been discussed in the specific area of product safety,[30] significant developments are occurring 'bottom-up', as, for example, advisory agencies discover that they must take account of the cross-border dimension in order to fulfil their tasks to inform the consumer of rights and remedies. For example, travellers through the Channel Tunnel have been presented with 'The Consumer's Travel Companion', a pamphlet which is aimed at providing simple, basic information to British tourists in France and French tourists in Britain. It is written in both languages. It was prepared by the Agence Européenne d'Information sur la Consommation (AEIC) in Lille, which is one of the Euroguichets. Other bodies involved were the UK-based Consumers in Europe Group and the UK's Office of Fair Trading, and financial support was forthcoming from the European Commission, the Region Nord Pas de Calais and Le Shuttle, the Eurotunnel group. It is a small example of the possibilities of cooperation between Commission and authorities within the member states at central, regional and local levels.

In 1995 the Commission proposed a Directive based on Article 100a on injunctions for the protection of consumers' interests.[31] This measure would coordinate national provisions relating to actions for an injunction which may be brought with regard to certain unfair commercial practices and would secure mutual recognition of the entities entitled to bring such actions. The introduction of such a procedure would be a potentially significant step in the consumer field beyond the normal assumption that existing national procedures should be employed in order to implement and enforce Directives. It could improve enforcement in practice, especially in relation to pernicious practices that exert a cross-border impact in particular, but it

[29.] Pricing it at 9 ECU seems likely to restrict its accessibility to consumers.
[30.] Chapter 7. [31.] COM (95) 712.

remains to be seen whether political support is forthcoming.

Closer to the level of the individual consumer, the Commission followed up its 1993 Green Paper in 1996 with a communication entitled 'Action plan on consumer access to justice and the settlement of consumer disputes in the internal market'.[32] This is shaped by comments made on the 1993 Green Paper. The Commission repeats the view that tackling problems of access to justice involves local, national and European agencies. It adds that 'in consonance notably with the provisions of Article 129a and the principle of subsidiarity, Community measures will of necessity be restricted'. The Commission states its determination to maintain support for pilot projects designed to improve access to justice and to help with information distribution. It places special priority on assembling a guide to legal aid practice in the member states. It is also concerned to improve knowledge about practical dispute settlement in the member states.

Information gathered from studies reveals the alarming cost of consumer access to justice. The average cost (court costs plus lawyers' fees) of in-court settlement of a dispute between two parties domiciled in two different member states over an amount equivalent to 2,000 ECU corresponds to approximately 2,500 ECU for the plaintiff. The average duration of such a case before a lower court ranges between 23.5 and 29.2 months. Both statistics assume the case is basically uncomplicated. Naturally, such figures conceal different trends in different states, but they suggest a likelihood of consumer reluctance to pursue a cross-border complaint and therefore a potential dissuasive effect on cross-border shopping.

The Commission plans to promote out-of-court procedures. It also aims to simplify access to court procedures, although it is understandably cautious about proposing harmonization as such, preferring the notion of producing a standard European form for intra-Community disputes. The Commission also mentions the possibility of class actions and related procedures,[33] but appears to be wary of disagreements among the member states in this area. The sensitivity felt towards proposed Community intrusion into national civil procedure appears likely to endure.

---

32. COM (96) 13.
33. Cf. T. Bourgoignie (ed.), *Group actions and consumer protection* (Brussels, Story Scientia, 1992).

CHAPTER NINE

Evaluating Community consumer policy

The history of consumer law has much in common with the development of other areas of Community regulatory activity. Out of an original Treaty pattern which promised little other than the indirect fruits of the process of market integration, a network of Community policies affecting the consumer have developed. The European Court has shaped a perception of the consumer in assessing the permissibility of national techniques of market regulation, including consumer protection, which impede the integrative process. The political institutions have been responsible for a soft law framework for the development of consumer policy. Moreover, the programme of harmonization of laws has involved Community legislative activity in the field of consumer protection. Although harmonization is constitutionally driven by the imperatives of economic integration, it leads to a Community pattern of laws affecting the consumer interest. Since the entry into force of the Single European Act in 1987, the constitutional link between internal market policy and consumer protection (if not the detailed elaboration of the relationship) has been beyond doubt, thanks to Article 100a(3).

Comparable comments could be directed at the evolution of other Community policies which have an ambiguous connection with the process of market integration, in part as a result of their absence from the text of the original Treaty of Rome. Environmental policy and cultural policy provide other examples of policies that have emerged from a combination of judicial decision making in the area of negative law, soft law and harmonization policy. Matters such as education and training and social policy were not wholly absent from the original Treaty, but the impact of Community law in such areas has far exceeded the expectations that would be engendered by a reading of the relevant, rather bare, Treaty provisions, so these sectors, too, offer illustrations of the tendency of Community law and policy to develop by accretion over time.

This book has portrayed this pattern of growth of consumer law and policy as inevitable in the light of the impact of the process of market integration through law on a wide range of economic and social policies pursued at national level. The explicit terms of the Treaty cannot in any formal sense constrain the evolution of Community law and policy because of the dynamism which is inherent in the Community's mission, expressed in the EC Treaty's Preamble 'to lay the foundations of an ever closer union among the peoples of Europe'.

However, a number of undercurrents pervade this inquiry. Although there is a collection of EC legal material which affects the consumer, is it straining analytical coherence to describe this as 'consumer policy'? Is it really no more than an erratically conceived grouping of general trade practices law? If this is so, it would not defeat the perception that there is a Community notion of the consumer, but it would suggest that this notion takes different and perhaps quite irreconcilable shapes depending on the context in which it arises, because the issue of consumer policy, *per se*, is unconnected with mainstream Community activity. Such an inquiry is especially important in the light of the inclusion at Maastricht of a new Title on consumer protection. Article 129a is a constitutional step beyond Article 100a(3), in that it offers scope for regarding consumer policy as more than an indirect consequence of internal market policy. But the terms of Article 129a are rather vague. They have been little used by the legislature since entry into force on 1 November 1993 and the Court was wholly unpersuaded by the argument that the new emphasis on consumer protection revealed by Article 129a should cause it to accept that Directives are capable of horizontal direct effect.[1] So what exactly might consumer policy in the EC mean, now that it has been 'constitutionalized' in the Treaty? And what will be the impact of the creation in 1995 of a new Directorate-General in the Commission with responsibility for consumer protection alone?

These are questions about the content of EC consumer policy

[1.] Chapter 8, p. 145.

, as such. But what level of regulatory intensity is appropriate? This relates to unresolved debates about the potential for a consumer policy that is autonomous, as distinct from the process of building and maintaining an internal market. But they are also questions that concern the relationship between Community consumer policy and policies pursued at national level: do these compete with or complement each other? The use of the minimum harmonization formula is well established in consumer Directives and is expressly included in Article 129a(3). The widespread use of soft law also represents a Community policy which is shaped by its environment, rather than simply pre-empting national action by occupying the field. The starting point of the objective of the 'level playing field' remains helpful, but today the Community has to face debates about how much *less* than a level playing field it should be (a competition between regulators, based on persisting national diversity and mutual recognition?) and how much *more* than a level playing field it should be (how much regulation should be introduced at Community level to cope with social and economic consequences of integration?). These are difficulties which pervade the modern Community, engaged on a path of geographic and functional expansion.

The variety of harmonization measures discussed in this book disclose a range of different techniques and assumptions. One can classify the measures according to a number of different categories. Some have an impact on public law, others on private law. The latter category is the smaller, but, of late, developments affecting private law have accelerated. Some Directives concern the health and safety of consumers, whereas others govern the economic interests of consumers. The former category was the subject of more intense activity in the early years of consumer-related EC law, but legislation affecting economic interests has subsequently become more prevalent. Some measures introduce prohibitions, others adopt techniques of information provision.

Such classifications, which may be traced throughout this book, are valuable yet dangerous. Their value lies in their capacity to provide a thematic framework within which to examine the pattern of the law in detail. Their danger lies in the risk that they may lead one to over-state academically attractive thematic order where there is, in practice, none. It is submitted that the measures which form the subject matter of most of this book do not on their own form a comprehensive package of consumer protection law. Their uneasy relationship with the disparate patterns of national consumer law, combined with their overt concern to advance market integration, render such coherence inconceivable. But it is also submitted that the Community has developed policies in the consumer field which are more sophisticated than mere technical harmonization of laws. Community consumer law reflects perceptions of market failure which rob the consumer of an efficiently operating economy. Intransparency, for example, prompts a response through mandatory information disclosure, which has become a *leitmotif* of legislative policy in relation to the protection of economic interests. And the 'Europeanization' of private law is, at least, a potential development of yet deeper impact. But the absence in this book of any attempt to define 'the consumer' is entirely deliberate. Consumer policy in the EC is a mix of legal techniques. But the same is true of consumer policy at national level.

Recent initiatives have made play of the notion that consumer protection at EC level is capable of instilling confidence in the cross-border consumer and thereby invigorating market integration through transfrontier shopping. In the past, the rationale for harmonization has normally been based on the perception that business needs a common set of rules in order to be encouraged to take advantage of the internal market. The consumer is, in such circumstances, merely the passive beneficiary of trade liberalization. However, recently a new attitude has begun to take shape, which views the level playing field from the perspective of the consumer. The rationale lies in the perception that the consumer needs the confidence of a minimum set of Community-wide protective rules if he or she is going to be willing to shop without reference to borders.

The recitals to Directive 93/13 on unfair terms in consumer contracts[2] explain that, 'generally speaking, consumers do not know the rules of law which, in member states other than their own, govern contracts for the sale of goods or services'. It is then claimed, rather more speculatively, that 'this lack of awareness may deter them from direct transactions for the purchase of goods or services in another member state'. The Green Paper on Consumer Guarantees[3] is similarly strongly motivated by the need

---

2. Chapter 4.   3. Chapter 4.

to create a minimum common floor of EC consumer rights in order to invest consumers with confidence in the operation of the market. It declares that 'Cross-border shopping can only flourish if the consumer knows he will enjoy the same guarantee and after-sales service conditions no matter where the supplier is located'.[4]

This new awareness that the consumer is a key player in the successful construction of an internal market also emerges strongly from the 1992 Sutherland Report. This identifies consumer uncertainty about effective law enforcement as a major obstacle to the practical realization of the internal market. The report insists on the need to create confidence to overcome such uncertainty. Relevant areas of activity should include both substantive law and access to justice.

This new focus on the need for a floor of common Community protective rules, in order to give the consumer confidence to take the internal market seriously, goes far beyond the disparate motivations that have prompted the growth of an indirect EC consumer policy in the past. Naturally, views may differ on the validity of the assertion that lack of legal knowledge dissuades cross-border consumer activity. The extent to which Community legislation can truly serve to resolve that perceived problem is also questionable. Nevertheless, inducing consumer confidence in the market is at least a candidate principle for developing new initiatives in the future. Both Articles 100a and 129a seem capable of providing legal bases for relevant proposals. In principle, subsidiarity under Article 3b does not obstruct such notions, for these are developments that can convincingly be presented as achievable only through Community action. The Green Paper on consumer guarantees provides an illustration. Market integration and consumer protection are both Community activities, according to Article 3 EC. A European legal guarantee would contribute in both areas by encouraging a consumer to be confident enough to cross borders. Leaving the matter to national systems would cause legal diversity and uncertainty among consumers. It is therefore efficient for the Community to act in conformity with Article 3b. The same analysis could be used in relation to questions of access to justice in the cross-border context. Where access to justice and

4. At p. 5.

information provision cannot effectively be developed by the member states, the matter may be regarded as more effectively achieved by Community action. There is now considerable constitutional flexibility enjoyed by the Community in the field of consumer policy. This isolates the critical determinant in the future shaping of EC consumer policy as political will among the member states.

Further reading and sources of information

The leading European journals in the English language which specialise in consumer law are the *Journal of Consumer Policy*, published by Kluwer, *Consumer Law Journal* (Sweet and Maxwell) and *Consumer Policy Review* (Consumers' Association). All include relevant articles, notes and summaries of recent developments. To varying degrees, all adopt a focus that is wider than law alone and wider than the EC alone. The German *Verbraucher und Recht*, published by Werner-Verlag, also deserves mention for its up-to-date coverage. Consumer issues are also frequently discussed in other, more general law reviews at domestic and European and, less often, international levels. Most law publishers have consumer law lists and EC law lists. However, this book is the first in English dealing with EC consumer law and policy as such. For readers of German, Norbert Reich's *Europäisches Verbraucherrecht* (Nomos, 1996) should not go unmentioned.

The Centre de Droit de la Consommation in the Université Catholique de Louvain-la-Neuve (Collège Thomas More, Place Montesquieu 2, B-1348 Louvain-la-Neuve, Belgium) has published a number of titles dealing with aspects of EC consumer law and policy. It hosts an annual Summer Programme in EC Consumer Law, offering intensive tuition over a ten day period in English and French by experts from all over Europe.

The institutions of the European Union are seeking to improve transparency *inter alia* by electronic means. They are making increasing use of the Internet. The main home page for the EU institutions, run by the Commission, can be found at http://europa.eu.int. The Consumer Policy Directorate General can be located at http://www.cec.lu/en/comm/spc/spc.html. It seems probable that these sites will be rapidly expanded and improved and are likely to become the most reliable source of up-to-date information on EC initiatives. The Consumer Policy Directorate General also produces a regular newsletter containing information about its own activities and those of national consumer bodies. This is 'INFO-C'. The address of DG XXIV, 'Consumer Policy' is European Commission, DG XXIV Consumer Policy, rue de la Loi 200, B-1049 Brussels, Belgium.

Other useful addresses include Consumers in Europe Group, 24 Tufton Street, London, SW1P 3RB; BEUC, Bureau Européenne des Unions de Consommateurs, Avenue de Tervuren 36, Box 4, 1040 Brussels, Belgium; and National Consumer Council, 20 Grosvenor Gardens, London, SW1W 0DH.

Bibliography

Argiros, G., 'The EEC Directive on General Product Safety' [1994/1] LIEI 125, 1994.

Askham, T., and A. Stoneham, *EC Consumer Safety*, London, Butterworths, 1994.

Barnard C., and S. Deakin, 'Social Policy in Search of a Role' in A. Caiger and D. Floudas, *1996 Onwards*, Chichester, Wiley Chancery, 1996.

Bourgoignie, T., 'The 1985 Council Directive on product liability and its implementation in the member states of the European Union' in M. Goyens (ed.), *Directive 85/374/EEC on product liability: ten years after*, Louvain-la-Neuve, Centre de Droit de la Consommation, 1996.

—— (ed.), *Group actions and consumer protection*, Brussels, Story Scientia, 1992.

Bourgoignie, T., and D. Trubek, *Consumer Law, Common Markets and Federalism*, Berlin, De Gruyter, 1987.

Brandner, H., and P. Ulmer, 'The Community Directive on Unfair Terms in Consumer Contracts' 28 CMLRev 615, 1991.

Brittan, Sir Leon, Institutional Development of the EC' Public Law 567, 1992.

Caiger, A., and D. Floudas (eds), *1996 Onwards*, Chichester, Wiley Chancery, 1996.

Carlier, J. Y., *Guide des litiges transfrontaliéres*, Paris, Institut National de la Consommation, 1995.

Cecchini, P., *The European Challenge: 1992, the Benefits of a Single Market*, Aldershot, Wildwood House, 1988.

Close, G., 'The Legal Basis for the Consumer Protection Programme of the EEC and the Priorities for Action' 8 ELRev 221, 1983.

Collins, A. M., 'Commercial Speech and the Free Movement of Goods and Services at Community Law' in J. O'Reilly (ed.), *Human Rights and Constitutional Law*, Dublin, Butterworths, 1992.

Collins, H., 'European Private Law and Cultural Identity of States' 3 European Review of Private Law 353, 1995.

—— 'Good Faith in European Contract Law' 14 Oxford JLS 229, 1994.

Cremona, M., 'Freedom of Movement of Financial Services' in A. Caiger and D. Floudas (eds), *1996 Onwards*, Chichester, Wiley Chancery, 1996.

Cross, E., 'Pre-emption of Member State Law in the European Economic Community: a Framework for Analysis' 29 CMLRev 447, 1992.

Curtin, D., and K. Mortelmans, 'Application and Enforcement of Community Law by the Memberstates: Actors in Search of a Third Generation Script' in D. Curtin and T. Heukels (eds), *Institutional Dynamics of a European Integration*, Dordrecht, Martinus Nijhoff, 1994.

Curtin, D., and T. Heukels (eds), *Institutional Dynamics of a European Integration*, Dordrecht, Martinus Nijhoff, 1994.

Daintith, T., (ed.), *Implementing EC Law in the UK: Structures for Indirect Rule*, Chichester, Wiley Chancery, 1995.

Dehousse, 'Community Competence: Are there Limits to Growth?' in R. Dehousse (ed.), *Europe After Maastricht*, Munich, Law Books, 1994.

Ehlerman, C.-D., 'How Flexible is Community Law? An Unusual Approach to the Concept of "Two Speeds"' Michigan Law Rev 1274, 1984.

Emiliou, N., 'Opening Pandora's Box: The Legal Basis of Community Measures before the Court of Justice' 19 ELRev 488, 1994.

Evans, A., 'European Competition Law and Consumers: the Article 85(3) Exemption' ECLR 425, 1981.

Fallon, M., and F. Maniet (eds), *Product Safety and control processes in the European Community*, Brussels, Story Scientia/CDC, 1990.

Gibson, L., 'Subsidiarity: the Implications for Consumer Policy' 16 JCP 323, 1993.

Gormley, L., 'Reasoning Renounced? The remarkable judgment in *Keck and Mithouard*' European Business Law Rev 63, 1994.

Goyens, M., 'EC Policy with regard to Consumer Redress' Consum LJ 35, 1995.

—— (ed.), *Directive 85/374/EEC on product liability: ten years after*, Louvain-la-Neuve, Centre de Droit de la Consommation, 1996.

Hartkamp, A., et al (eds), *Towards a European Civil Code*, Dordrecht, Martinus Nijhoff, 1994.

Hartley, T., *The Foundations of EC Law*, Oxford, Clarendon Press, 3rd edn, 1994.

Hodges, C. J. S., *Product Liability: European Laws and Practice*, London, Sweet and Maxwell, 1993.

Hoffman, D., 'Product safety in the internal market: the proposed Community emergency procedure', in M. Fallon and F. Maniet (eds), *Product Safety and control processes in the European Community*, Brussels, Story Scientia/CDC, 1990.

Hondius, E., 'The Reception of the Directive on Unfair Contract Terms by the Member States' 3 European Review of Private Law 241, 1995.

House of Lords Select Committee on the European Communities 22nd Report, 1977–8.

Howells, G., *Comparative Product Liability*, Aldershot, Dartmouth, 1992.

—— 'Product Liability' in A. Hartkamp et al (eds), *Towards a European Civil Code*, Dordrecht, Martinus Nijhoff, 1994.

Howells, G., and S. Weatherill, *Consumer Protection Law*, Aldershot, Dartmouth, 1995.

Hutchinson, A., 'Money Talk: Against Constitutionalizing (Commercial) Speech' 17 Canadian Business Law Journal 2, 1990.

Joerges, C., 'Social Regulation and the Legal Structure of the EEC', in B. Stauder (ed.), *La Sécurité des produits de consommation*, Zürich, Schulthess, 1992.

Kelly, P., and R. Attree, *European Product Liability*, London, Butterworths, 1992.

Krämer, L., *EEC Consumer Law*, Brussels, Story Scientia, 1986.

Kye, C., 'Environmental Law and the Consumer in the EU' 7 Journal of Environmental Law 31, 1995.

Lando, O., 'Principles of European Contract Law: An Alternative or a Precursor of European Legislation' *Rabels Zeitschrift* 261, 1992.

Legrand, P., 'European Legal Systens are not Converging' 45 ICLQ 52, 1996.

Ludwig, B., *Irreführende und vergleichende Werbung in der EG*, Baden-Baden, Nomos, 1995.

Maxeiner, J., and P. Schotthöfer, *Advertising Law in Europe and North America*, Dordrecht, Kluwer, 1992.

McGee, A., and S. Weatherill, 'The Evolution of the Single Market – Harmonisation or Liberalisation?' 53 Modern Law Rev 578, 1990.

Micklitz, H.-W., *Internationales Produktsicherheitrecht*, Baden-Baden, Nomos, 1995.

—— (ed.), *Rechtseinheit oder Rechtsvielfalt in Europa?*, Baden-Baden, Nomos, 1996.

—— *Post Market Control of Consumer Goods*, Baden-Baden, Nomos, 1990.

Micklitz, H.-W., T. Roethe and S. Weatherill (eds), *Federalism and Responsibility: a Study on Product Safety Law and Practice in the European Community*, London, Graham and Trotman, 1994.

Mildred, M., 'The Impact of the Directive in the United Kingdom', in M. Goyens (ed.), *Directive 85/374/EEC on product liability: ten years after*, Louvain-la-Neuve, Centre de Droit de la Consommation, 1996.

Mortelmans, K., 'Minimum Harmonisation and Consumer Law' European Consumer Law Journal 2, 1988.

Newdick, C., 'The Development Risk Defence of the Consumer Protection Act 1987', Cambridge Law Journal 455, 1998.

—— 'Risk, Uncertainty and Knowledge in the Development Risks Defence' 20 Anglo-Am L Rev 309, 1991.

Piper, H., 'Zu den Auswirkungen des EG-Binnenmarktes auf das deutsche Recht gegen den unlauteren Wettbewerb' Wettbewerb in Recht und Praxis 685, 1992.

Prechal, S., *Directives in EC Law*, Oxford, OUP, 1995.

Reich, N., 'Competition Between Legal Orders: A New Paradigm of EC Law' 29 CMLRev 861, 1992.

—— *Europäisches Verbraucherrecht*, Baden-Baden, Nomos, 3rd edn, 1996.

—— 'The November Revolution of the European Court of Justice: Keck, Meng and Audi Revisited' 31 CMLRev 459, 1994.

—— 'Protection of Consumers' Economic Interests by the EC' 14 Sydney Law Rev 23, 1992.

Reynolds, F., Annotation, 110 LQR 1, 1994.

Schmitz, B., 'Advertising and Commercial Communications – Towards a Coherent and Effective EC Policy' 16 Journal of Consumer Policy 387, 1993.

Schricker, G., 'European Harmonization of Unfair Competition Law – a Futile Venture?' in *ICC (International Review of Industrial Property and Copyright Law)* 6/1991, 788, 1991.

Shapo, M., 'Comparing Products Liability: Concepts in European and American Law' 26 Cornell International Law Journal 279, 1993.

Skouris, W., (ed.), *Advertising and Constitutional Rights in Europe*, Baden-Baden, Nomos, 1994.

Sosnitza, O., *Wettbewerbsbeschränkungen durch die Rechtsprechung*, Baden-Baden, Nomos, 1995.

Stapleton, J., *Product Liability*, London, Butterworths, 1994.

Taupitz, J., *Europäische Privatrechtsvereinheitlichung heute und morgen*, Tübingen, JCB Mohr, 1993.

Tenreiro, M., 'The Community Directive on Unfair Terms and National Legal Systems' 3 European Review of Private Law 273, 1995.

Usher, J., *The Law of Money and Financial Services in the EC*, Oxford, OUP, 1994.

Vahrenwald, A., 'The Advertising Law of the EU' EIPR 279, 1996.

Van Empel, M., 'The 1992 Programme: Interaction between Legislator and Judiciary' [1992/2] LIEI 1, 1992.

Viitanen, K., 'Consumer Redress' Consum LJ 6, 1995.

Von Heydebrand und der Lasa, H.-C., 'Free Movement of Foodstuffs, Consumer Protection and Food Standards in the European Community: Has the Court of Justice got it wrong?' 16 ELRev 391, 1991.

Weatherill, S., 'The Evolution of European Consumer Law and Policy: from well-informed consumer to confident consumer', in H.-W. Micklitz (ed.), *Rechtseinheit oder Rechtsvielfalt in Europa?*, Baden-Baden, Nomos, 1996.

—— *Law and Integration in the European Union*, Oxford, OUP, 1995.

—— 'Playing Safe: the UK's Implementation of the Toy Safety Directive' in T. Daintith (ed.), *Implementing EC Law in the UK*, Chichester, Wiley Chancery, 1995.

—— 'Prospects for the Development of European Private Law through Europeanisation in the European Court of Justice' 3 European Review of Private Law 307, 1995.

—— 'The Reinvigoration of Community Product Safety Policy' 14 Journal of Consumer Policy 171, 1991.

—— 'The role of the informed consumer in EC Law and Policy' 2 Consumer Law J 49, 1994

Weatherill, S., and P. Beaumont, *EC Law*, London, Penguin Books, 2nd edn, 1995.

Weiler, J., 'The Transformation of Europe' 100 Yale LJ 2403, 1991.

Whiteford, E., 'Social Policy after Maastricht' 19 ELRev 202, 1993.

Wilhelmsson, T., 'Control of Unfair Contract Terms and Social Values: EC and Nordic Approaches' 16 JCP 435, 1993.

—— *Social Contract Law and European Integration*, Aldershot, Dartmouth, 1994.

Willett, C., 'Directive on Unfair Terms in Consumer Contracts' Consum LJ 114, 1994.

Index